Text copyright © Eleanor Zuercher 2009
Illustrations copyright © Ann Kronheimer 2009
The author asserts the moral right
to be identified as the author of this work

Published by
The Bible Reading Fellowship
15 The Chambers, Vineyard
Abingdon OX14 3FE
United Kingdom
Tel: +44 (0)1865 319700
Email: enquiries@brf.org.uk
Website: www.brf.org.uk

ISBN 978 1 84101 578 1
First published 2009
10 9 8 7 6 5 4 3 2 1 0

Acknowledgments
Unless otherwise stated, scripture quotations are taken from the
Contemporary English Version of the Bible published by HarperCollins
Publishers, copyright (c) 1991, 1992, 1995 American Bible Society.

A catalogue record for this book is available from the British Library

Printed in Singapore by Craft Print International Ltd

THROUGH THE YEAR
WITH JESUS!

A once-a-month children's programme
for small churches

Eleanor Zuercher

Eleanor Zuercher lives and works in a rural parish in the West Buckingham Benefice (a group of six rural parishes) where for the past five years she has been running workshops for children aged 3–12. Alongside this work, she oversees all the children's work for her parish as well as being involved in planning and taking services. Eleanor is married with a young family. Although she worked as a company secretary for many years, she has recently retrained as a teacher and is enjoying her new career teaching in a local Church of England primary school. Her first book for Barnabas, *Not Sunday, Not School!*, was published in 2006.

In memory of my father, Eric, and my mother, Beryl,
with love and thanks.

ACKNOWLEDGMENTS

My particular thanks go to the children of Acorns and Saplings, their families and especially the volunteer helpers and congregations of St Mary Magdalene in Tingewick and the rest of the West Buckingham Benefice, who allowed me to try out experimental activities on them; also Hanno, Crispin and Bertie, who have to humour me for much longer periods of time at a stretch.

CONTENTS

FOREWORD

What are the important things about our faith that we should share with children? Families are so busy, or put so much less importance on attending church regularly, that few children are brought to church weekly. This can mean that children gain patchy knowledge of the life of Jesus and the beliefs of the Church because they attend only occasionally.

This book provides a coherent approach to providing children with a framework of knowledge for faith. The monthly workshop approach means that children, and the adults helping, will learn about Jesus and what Christians believe as they have fun together. Some churches may only manage to run one of the workshops at each school holiday; others will find material here to stage a monthly club for children as well as an activity programme for the summer.

Each workshop stands alone and does not assume that children have previous knowledge. The crafts and activities are fun, and each session ends with ideas to help children to pray. The material is flexible so that the organizers can work to their strengths and choose activities to utilize the time available.

In *Through the Year with Jesus!* Eleanor Zuercher shares the way she has developed monthly midweek activity sessions for children. In her parish, monthly workshops have attracted many more children than a traditional weekly Sunday school. Her experience reflects national research which suggests that more than 40 per cent of children attending church activities do so midweek rather than on Sunday.

Whether you want to use this book to work with children or to run workshops for families, be inspired to try the lovely ideas in the programmes. I pray that God will bless you as you share his good news with the children in your area.

Rona Orme, Children's Missioner, Diocese of Peterborough

HOW TO USE THIS BOOK

This book contains all you need to plan through-the-year workshop programmes for children, exploring themes surrounding the life of Jesus. There is material for eleven workshops (one for each month except August, if you wish) plus a five-day summer activity programme. Each programme is designed to last approximately two hours, although this timescale can be shortened or lengthened according to need. Each workshop contains:

★ Suggestions for Bible stories based on the theme
★ Suggestions for creating a display for the church
★ Craft activities
★ Games
★ Suggestions for prayer

The ideas are intended to be used on a pick-and-mix basis to help you create your own programme. Since so much depends on the age, interests and abilities of the children, you may find that activities will take longer or much less time. Therefore, the timings given are guidelines only. Activities could also be run simultaneously, so that the children move in groups from one activity to the next if time and space round the tables is short.

TIMING

Each activity is designed to last between 10 and 15 minutes. Sample plans for each workshop, showing an outline programme for younger and older children, can be found on the website: www.barnabasinchurches.org.uk/throughtheyearwithjesus.

The suggested activities for creating a display for the church are designed to last between 15 and 20 minutes. However, depending on the age and ability of the children, more time can be spent on them if required.

ADDITIONAL MATERIAL

Visit the Barnabas website, www.barnabasinchurches.org.uk, for additional material, including extra ideas and articles on integrating children's work into the wider congregation (especially important if your children meet at a time other than Sunday morning).

All the templates for the activities (see pages 183–191), as well as the sample plans for each workshop, can be downloaded free of charge from the website:

www.barnabasinchurches.org.uk/throughtheyearwithjesus

INTRODUCTION

THE RURAL CONTEXT

The material in this book is based on the experience of working with children in a rural context. However, many of the principles applied to the rural setting are equally relevant to an urban, suburban or larger town situation. Due to low numbers and the dispersion of the community, children's work in small rural communities can be immensely challenging, and it is often not possible to presuppose that the work can follow the traditional model of meeting each week on Sunday morning while the adults attend the morning service. Therefore, it is paramount to consider a range of concerns, which may, of course, also apply to non-rural situations. The concerns include:

* ★ The best day and time for your children's work.
* ★ The best place to hold your meetings.
* ★ The best mixture of activities.
* ★ Who will be responsible for which task.
* ★ How to advertise your club.
* ★ How to identify suitable sources of funding.
* ★ How to ensure that all child protection and health and safety measures are in place.
* ★ What to do about potential difficulties, such as lack of toilets or kitchen facilities.

OPPORTUNITIES AND ADVANTAGES

The challenge of working with a small number of children also provides an ideal opportunity for encouragement and reward. For example, small numbers mean that you will be able to get to know and serve individual children far better. Also, you have the advantage of being able to tailor your children's work to your own individual requirements.

Don't worry if you don't have a limitless expenses fund and all the state-of-the-art technology on the market. Concentrate instead on making your programmes imaginative, creative and unique. The enjoyment the children get out of your sessions will not depend on technology; that is only a means to an end. Also, if you are lacking a nicely furnished, carpeted, warm room, make sure you use the symbolism, images and atmosphere available in the building you do use—especially if it is the church. The church building is entirely different from any other the children are likely to enter on a regular basis. The children will appreciate that it is special, particularly if you make their time there special too.

Don't worry if you are unable to run a Sunday school on a Sunday morning. It is far better practice and richer in spiritual terms if the children are welcomed as part of the normal pattern of worship along with adult members of the congregation. Having the children present will also help adults and children to learn from each other in their understanding of faith and the Bible, so encourage your church leadership to ensure that provision is made to include children fully in Sunday worship.

Use your workshop times productively by keeping the teaching focused. Rather than coming to church on a regular basis, some children may only attend the monthly workshop, so this will be a golden opportunity for them to hear the basic stories of Christianity —perhaps for the first time.

PLANNING AND PREPARATION

As you would expect, if children's work is to be successful it needs careful planning and preparation. Some of the activities in this book require more preparation than others, but time spent in this area is always worthwhile. Make sure you give the children good-quality resources to use. It is a good idea to try out the ideas at home first, so that you know how they work and can show the children a finished example.

Alongside the workshop ideas, you may wish to add songs or percussion music to your programme. As well as using your own style of music and favourite songs, it is a good idea to find out what songs the children sing at school and use this information to enlarge your repertoire.

You will also need to give some consideration to the presentation of stories. This can be varied from programme to programme by using different storytelling methods. For example, you could use a child-friendly Bible translation, such as the Contemporary English Version, or a children's storytelling Bible, such as *The Barnabas Children's Bible* (Barnabas, 2007). Alternatively, you could tell the story using visual aids, actions, mime or drama, or by using the methodology of Godly Play (see www.godlyplay.org.uk).

INTEGRATING CHILDREN'S WORK WITHIN THE CHURCH AND COMMUNITY

One of the problems that may arise if your children's work does not operate on a Sunday morning is that the adult congregation may forget, or be unaware of, what is available for children. The ideas below should ensure that the profile is kept high and that everyone is encouraged to pray for the children's activities.

IDENTITY

Choose a suitable name for your group and display it prominently in the church building. For example, you could make a simple banner with the name painted on it and children's handprints to decorate it. Also, make sure there are articles and advertisements in your church magazine, using your group name.

CHILDREN'S COUNCIL

Having a link between the children and the church council (or your equivalent) is a very useful way to ensure that your church leaders are informed about the children's work. This can also serve as a valuable way of setting up communication links, but make sure that it is two-way communication. You might want to consider having your children's leader or a representative specifically for children and young people on the church council.

To make the communication process easier, you might consider setting up a children's council. Many schools have children's councils, so children are often used to being asked for and articulating their views. If children's opinions are sought and respected in schools and other contexts, churches need to make sure children are also given a voice in the church setting. A children's church council will give the children a chance to air their views, with regard to their own activities and to the life of the church as a whole. Adult members of the congregation may learn more about the spiritual maturity of children in their midst from this process than they might anticipate.

WORSHIP

If the children's activities are run outside normal service times, there is a danger that all-age worship may be put slightly lower on the list of priorities. To remedy this, and to remind the rest of the worshipping community about the children, it is important to ensure that children and their families can be welcomed at any service. Families need to have the opportunity to worship together, as well as provision being made for children to learn about faith together, with suitable activities and stories. Alongside the mainstream services, you may wish to find ways for the children also to make a special contribution to the celebration of a major festival.

LOCAL LINKS

Local organizations, of which your church is one, can provide useful links. For example, your local school might find the resource of your church building very useful, not only for the provision of the RE curriculum but also for holding large festival assemblies, attended by parents as well as children. Schools often invite professional people to take assemblies, and children's work leaders are likely candidates for an invitation. An added bonus to visiting the school is that pupils will get to know you and what you do. Word of mouth spreads quickly, and more children may be interested in coming to church-based activities and events. Also, the local school may be a willing source for items such as harvest gifts or displays to decorate the church.

Other organizations or clubs might be able to contribute specialist themes. For example, a flower arranger could help the children to create special church decorations or something for Mothering Sunday, someone from the historical society could talk to the children about the locality, a local artist could demonstrate different media, and so on.

LONGER-TERM PROJECTS

The children may enjoy being involved in slightly longer-term projects, such as producing their own version of the church guide. You could use the celebration of Pentecost as a starting point. Think about how the church is the people rather than the building, and invite the children to write and draw pictures about how different people contribute. Don't leave out the fascinating information about the building, but present it in a way that interests and involves the children. You could include a plan of the church and a treasure hunt, which sends them round the building looking for historical clues. A photograph of a stained-glass window could be traced to produce a colouring page for younger children. Include children's pictures and ideas mixed with photographs, and adult-produced maps and puzzles.

If you have any keen needleworkers, you could organize a design-a-kneeler project. If your church already has modern handmade kneelers and you know of a supplier, you simply need to measure your existing kneelers. If this is not the case, suppliers can be found via the Internet or through church journals. The children draw their design on a piece of A3 paper, using bold shapes and bright colours. Members of the adult congregation can then get involved by either stitching the designs or sponsoring the materials needed to make up the kneelers. The number of designs needed will depend on the number of stitchers and sponsors.

You can buy blank kneeler kits from suppliers and, using a squared grid, you will be able to work out how much of each coloured thread you will need to complete each design (not forgetting the sides, of course). You may need to adapt colours slightly for financial and aesthetic reasons. Transferring the design itself is easy: by placing the picture (or a copy of it) underneath the canvas, the design can be drawn on using felt-tipped pen. After a few weeks' work, you will have a series of colourful, original and highly unusual kneelers for your church. It's a nice idea to stitch the designer's name and age on the side of the kneeler for posterity. Fuller instructions for this activity can be found on the website: www.barnabasinchurches.org.uk/nsns (Click on 'Download the additional material'.)

CHILD PROTECTION AND HEALTH AND SAFETY

It is essential that you give both child protection and health and safety considerable attention. Your diocese (or equivalent) should be able to provide you with detailed information about what is required and how to go about fulfilling the requirements. It is vitally important that all your helpers have Criminal Records Bureau clearance and that you comply with the law by making sure that you run your sessions with proper attention to child protection and health and safety. Remember that the safeguards are there to protect not only the children who are in your care but also the adult helpers. Where you need assistance, ask for help. Obtaining clearance and holding records can easily be done by someone who wishes to support your children's work but may not be able to offer any physical help.

CHILD PROTECTION

Make sure you know how a child's disclosure of neglect or abuse at home should be handled. Check this with your diocese or equivalent. You are likely to find that there is someone nominated by the diocese to deal with these issues, which will avoid the situation (particularly destructive in close-knit communities) of neighbours being told, or perhaps the minister becoming aware of too much detail, which could make it difficult for him or her to continue to support the whole family. You may think that this scenario is unlikely in a small community where everyone appears to know everyone else's business, but we can never be sure what goes on behind closed doors. Waiting until after the disclosure has been made before finding out how it should have been handled is too late.

Check the requirements for the ratio of adults to children at your sessions. This will depend on the age of the children present, but you should always have enough adults to ensure that there are at least two present at any time with any child. Allow for the possibility of one adult having to leave the room for some reason: there should always be two left behind.

FIRST AID

At least one adult in each session should be a qualified first aider. If you need more people to be qualified, find out about local training courses for child first aid.

REGISTRATION

Make sure you have documentation giving information about the children in your care. A simple registration form will suffice. It should give the name and date of birth of the child, contact details including emergency contact details, information about any allergies and the name of the child's doctor. Permission for things like administration of first aid and taking of photographs could also be included.

A signing in and signing out form for parents as they drop and collect children will ensure that you know which children are present at any time. You will need to know exactly how and when this form will be completed so that it is always accurate. The form should include space for a parent to notify you if someone else will be collecting their children.

Sample forms for registration, parental consent and signing in and out can be found on the website:
www.barnabasinchurches.org.uk/nsns (Click on 'Download the additional material'.)

HEALTH AND SAFETY

Carry out a risk assessment by viewing the building or room(s) you will be using from a child's point of view. Take particular note of doors that may need to be watched to ensure that children don't escape during the session.

If you are using an ancient church building, be aware of steep stone steps, unguarded heaters, things that are shouting out to be climbed, or other hazards. Such hazards may not preclude the use of the building, but some will need to be dealt with, for example, by placing secure guards around heaters and designating certain areas as out-of-bounds. No room can ever be completely safe, but you must take every precaution to safeguard the children in your care.

Make sure that the electrical checks on wiring and equipment, and the fire extinguisher checks, are all up to date and that you have appropriate insurance cover. Check this with your PCC or governing council if you are unsure.

Some of the activities in this book suggest lighting candles, so for these you will need to make sure that children keep a safe distance. In addition, you should have fire precaution materials to hand (water or sand), and a candle extinguisher.

Finally, make sure you know where the fire exits are, and that they are accessible in the event of fire.

THEMED PROGRAMMES

Theme 1

BAPTISM:
THE NAME GAME

KEY BIBLE FOCUS: MATTHEW 3:13–17

Although many children may be familiar with the term 'baptism', some may not have experienced a service of baptism or seen photographs of their own baptism. The symbolism associated with baptism is particularly rich and worth exploring to help children gain an insight into God's care for us.

BIBLE STORIES

The story of Jesus' baptism at the very beginning of his ministry provides an ideal introduction to the theme. The story can be told by using a children's storytelling Bible, such as *The Barnabas Children's Bible*, or a modern version of the Bible, such as the Contemporary English Version. Alternatively, the story can be told using visual aids, such as a story cloth and simple figures. You may also wish to tell the story using a simple version of the baptism liturgy, lighting a candle for each child present and using a doll to show how baptism is performed. There is a helpful script for a re-enactment of a baptism in the book *Living Church* by Murray McBride (Barnabas, 2006).

DISPLAYS FOR THE CHURCH

You could make a display using the dove mobiles activity below. However, the range of items used in the craft activities picks up the symbols of water, oil, the dove and the scallop shell, all of which are key symbols associated with baptism. These craft items would therefore make an ideal display to set up in the church building. You might also include artefacts used in the storytelling and a printed copy of the story itself. The display could be placed on a table covered with a blue cloth, or set up in front of a display board decorated with photographs of the children's work.

CRAFT ACTIVITIES

DOVES MOBILE

You will need: pre-cut dove shapes with slots cut in them (see template on page 183); strong cotton thread; hole punch; coloured paper for wings; garden sticks; felt-tipped pens or collage materials; PVA glue.

Chat about it

The dove is a symbol of God's Holy Spirit, which was seen to alight on Jesus as he came up out of the water after his baptism by John the Baptist.

Make it

Give each child a dove shape and ask them to decorate their doves using felt-tipped pens or collage materials. Make sure they keep the wing slot free. Fold the paper for the wings concertina-style and thread the folded paper through the wing slot. Open the folds out on either side to make the wings. Punch a hole in each dove as marked, and thread with cotton. Hang the finished doves from the garden sticks, tying them at different heights to create a mobile. For the wings, paper that has a different colour on each side can be very effective.

PAINTED SHELLS

You will need: scallop shells; acrylic paint; water; brushes.

Chat about it

Scallop shells were used as an emblem for Christian pilgrims in the Middle Ages and a shell is often used in baptism to pour water over the person being baptized. Once a person is baptized, he or she becomes a Christian pilgrim, seeking to follow Jesus.

Make it

You may be able to obtain scallop shells from a local fishmonger, or look out for them on the beach or in tourist shops in seaside holiday resorts. You will need to wash the shells thoroughly and dry them. Invite the children to decorate the shells using acrylic paint. They may find it easier to follow the grain of the shell than to make patterns across the grain. Older children may wish to attempt a picture across the grain, but younger children may enjoy following the grain with different colours and patterns. Allow time for the shells to dry before giving them to the children to take home.

MARBLING

> **You will need**: a water tray; water; marbling ink (available from craft shops); paper; plastic spoons.

Chat about it

Water and oil are both key symbols in baptism. Water symbolizes purity and sustenance (washing and living). Oil is used to anoint the baptism candidate, marking him or her as a member of God's family. It is also a symbol of the Holy Spirit.

Make it

Pour some water into the tray so that it is roughly 2–3cm deep. Ask each child to write their name on a piece of paper. In turn, each child will need to choose which colour inks they want to use. (It is best to use no more than three colours for each piece of paper.) Add a dose of each of the chosen coloured inks and give the water a very gentle swirl with a spoon if required. Then invite the child to lay the paper very gently on top of the water. Remove the paper after a couple of seconds, allowing the water to drip back into the tray. Put the paper to one side to dry. It is a good idea to take a second 'copy' to use up any remaining ink before the next child has his or her turn. You will need to experiment before the session starts so that you can judge how much ink you need for each paper.

OIL PASTEL PICTURES

You will need: oil pastels; good-quality paper.

Chat about it

The Holy Spirit is the third person in the Trinity. Explain to the children how God the Father, God the Son and God the Holy Spirit were all present at Jesus' baptism.

Make it

Show the children how to experiment with blending colours on the paper and smudging them to obtain interesting effects. Invite them to make some pictures connected to the symbols of baptism (such as oil or water), or showing their own ideas about how God's Holy Spirit became visible at Jesus' baptism.

ILLUMINATED NAMES

You will need: book of babies' names; paper; ink; small brushes (alternatively, you might wish to use tempura paint or gel pens).

Chat about it

Discuss with the children why we have names. Talk about surnames or family names; perhaps some children will have been named after other members of their family. Then talk about the fact that names often have a significant meaning. Use the name book to look up the meanings of the children's names. If anyone's name isn't in the book, the child might know an interesting story to go with his or her name.

With older children, you might like to take the discussion further by talking about what they would like to be called and why—concentrating particularly on the meaning of names. Then you might ask each child to think of an appropriate name for someone else in the group. Make sure that they consider good qualities only. Children might want to make up their own names for their friends to indicate their positive characteristics.

Make it

Show the children a book of illuminated manuscripts and look at how the initial letter or word is often decorated and embellished. If you are using tempura paints, older children could help to mix them. While you are mixing, explain that tempura was used before there were oil paints, and artists often had their own recipes for the various colours. Invite the children to make an illuminated picture of their name using the chosen materials. They could add things to the picture that are precious to them, or pictures of important events in their lives, their homes or school or friends.

STAINED-GLASS WINDOW CANDLES

You will need: black card; cellophane or tissue paper; glue sticks; scissors.

Chat about it

Remind the children that candles are given at baptism to the newly baptized person as a symbol of Christ's light in their life.

Make it

In advance, cut a candle design stencil (see page 184) out of the card. Invite the children to glue pieces of tissue paper or cellophane to the back of the stencil. Cellophane will give a clearer, brighter colour; tissue paper will diffuse the light more readily. Display the candles in a window for a stained-glass effect.

GAMES

BUBBLES

You will need: bubble mixture and blowers (one per child).

Chat about it

Think about the times when we find bubbles, such as when we are washing or cleaning our teeth. Remind the children that part of the symbolism of baptism is about spiritual washing.

Play it

Playing with bubbles is always irresistible and the idea is really to let the children have fun. Either allow the children to play freely with the bubbles or set up competitions, such as seeing who can blow the biggest bubble, the most bubbles in one go, the bubble that lasts longest or the bubble that floats highest. Make sure that the children observe basic safety measures, such as not pushing each other or indulging in horseplay.

WATER-CARRYING RACES

You will need: water; containers.

Chat about it

Talk to the children about how water is used in baptism to symbolize spiritual washing: the person being baptized shows a desire to turn away from wrongdoing and follow Jesus. Remind the children that in some parts of the world (including the Holy Land) water is scarce and therefore a precious commodity.

Play it

If your session takes place in the summer, it may be possible to go outside and hold water-carrying races. The idea is simply that children carry as much water as they can from one end of the course to the other in various containers as quickly as possible. Fast runners could be handicapped with leaky containers!

PRAYERS

BUBBLES

You will need: bubble mixture and blowers.

As well as generating great excitement, bubbles can also be used for prayers. Blow bubbles in the thinking time between sections of prayer, and watch them float away. (If you are using bubble-blowing as a game, it might be wise not to expect the children to behave more seriously with them only minutes later in prayer time!)

PRAYING WITH WATER

You will need: water; a container such as a font or glass bowl.

A font makes a wonderful focus for prayer, but if you don't have access to a font, a glass bowl will be fine. Fill the font or bowl with water. Talk about the children's own baptism, whether it is past or still to come (you will need to be sensitive to those children who have not been baptized), and its importance. Invite those present to come to the water and dip their fingers in. Let them think about what a wonderful part of creation water is. If they wish, they could make the sign of the cross on their own foreheads.

ACTIVE CONFESSION

In each line in the confession below, perform the action indicated by the words in the line.

Leader: When we come to say sorry to God, we can say it in a very special way.
First of all, we wash our hands for the wrong things we have done this week.

All mime washing hands.

Leader: Then we gently wash our eyes for the wrong things we have seen.

All mime washing eyes.

Reproduced with permission from *Through the Year with Jesus!* published by BRF 2009 (978 1 84101 578 1)
www.barnabasinchurches.org.uk

Leader: Then we wash our ears for the wrong things we have listened to.

All mime washing ears.

Leader: Then we wash our mouths for the wrong things we have said.

All mime washing mouths.

Leader: Then we very gently wash our minds for the wrong things we have thought.

All mime washing minds by rubbing forehead.

Leader: Then we gently wash our hearts for the wrong things we have felt.

All mime washing hearts by rubbing chest.

Leader: When we say sorry to God, he forgives us for all the times we have turned away from him and wraps us in the big, warm towel of his love.

All mime being wrapped up in a fluffy towel.

Leader: Thank you, Lord God, for making us clean.

All: Amen

Reproduced with permission from *Through the Year with Jesus!* published by BRF 2009 (978 1 84101 578 1)
www.barnabasinchurches.org.uk

Theme 2

FAITH:
MUSTARD SEEDS
AND MULBERRY TREES

KEY BIBLE FOCUS: LUKE 17:5–6

Faith is central to Christian belief, so it is important to explore with the children what it means, not only in general terms but also for them as individuals. For the children to see the way that the leaders model faith, and the way it affects their lives, is of great importance. The Bible focus is an excellent way to introduce the theme and promote discussion through a few short verses. Have some mustard seeds for the children to look at and a picture of a tree—or perhaps even refer to a real tree that the children can see growing outside. It is quite effective to place a tiny seed in each child's hand so that they can see for themselves how small a mustard seed is.

BIBLE STORIES

There are lots of stories in the Gospels that illustrate faith. For example, the story of Peter's denial (Luke 22:54–62) could be linked with the story of Jesus' response after the resurrection (John 21:15–19). Alternatively, the story of the centurion's servant (Luke 7:1–10) would also be very appropriate. You could tell these stories using books and pictures, from memory or with visual materials. As it is the impact of faith on our lives that is important, using drama techniques to tell the stories would also be very effective. Perhaps you could try 'hot-seating' Peter (ask one child to be Peter while the others ask questions about why he denied Jesus and what it felt like when he saw Jesus again). You could do some role play, asking the children to develop the conversation or scene that might have taken place in the story of the centurion's servant. Asking just a few children to act out certain parts of a story to the rest of the group can also be really effective.

DISPLAYS FOR THE CHURCH

ACORN TRIPTYCH

You will need: three pieces of strong card or fabric, such as hessian, each measuring approximately 75cm x 1m; simple shapes of an acorn, a sapling and an oak tree in full leaf; fabric or acrylic paints; sponges; oak leaf-shaped stencils; PVA glue; green card or fabric; fabric scraps in differing textures and shades of brown; white wool; masking tape; a suitable caption such as 'We are growing in faith'.

A triptych is a picture divided into three sections, which are hinged together. The middle panel is often the largest and most important of the three pieces. The triptych was an important style in early Christian art and can often be seen on the altar paintings of older church buildings. This makes it a very appropriate art form for a display about faith in your church building.

Begin by talking to the children about faith as something that is continually developing, changing and growing. The way our faith develops depends on the people we get to know and the experiences we have both of God and of other people. Sometimes faith might seem to grow very slowly, and sometimes it might grow very quickly. Although we need to take an active part in the way our faith grows (we need to want to explore and develop it), a lot depends on God. Lots of people (including Jesus) have explained faith as being like a plant growing.

Before the session, prepare the background by attaching the acorn, sapling and mature oak tree to the background pieces (one to each piece). If you are using card, the shapes can be glued; if you are using fabric, you will need to back each piece with iron-on fabric bonding and iron them in place. Show the children the prepared background fabric. Depending on the number of children you have and how much time you have allowed, you may have all the children contributing to each panel or groups of children working on one panel each.

The first panel shows an acorn in the soil, just germinating and beginning to sprout. Invite the children to use sponge painting to add the soil around the ready-prepared acorn shape. Paint in creatures that might live in the soil, such as worms, centipedes and beetles. With some green card or fabric, add a small shoot poking through the soil and use white wool to create some wispy roots.

The middle panel shows the acorn growing into a small tree, or sapling. The basic shape of the sapling will already be in place. Invite the children to use oak leaf-shaped stencils and sponge painting techniques to add some leaves to the plant. If you are running your session at an appropriate time of the year, you could try taking leaf prints from actual oak leaves. Make sure sponges are almost dry before painting, otherwise the paint will run under the edge of the stencil and blur the line. Take care as the stencils are applied and removed to ensure that the outlines remain clear.

The third panel shows a larger, mature tree. The shape of the trunk and branches will already be in place. Invite the children to use different fabric scraps to make textured bark for the trunk. Also use sponges to make foliage around the branches.

Make the triptych by attaching the three panels to each other with masking tape (if you have used card). If your triptych is on fabric, you could either stitch the panels together or hang them separately, but alongside each other. Attach your caption to the middle panel to explain what the display is about.

To adapt the design, the oak tree could easily be replaced with a different growing plant, such as a sunflower. In this case, the first panel would show the sunflower seed, the middle panel the growing plant and the third panel the fully grown flower and seed head.

Place the finished triptych on a table, or hang it on a wall if you have used fabric. You could add to the display by placing some real plants on the table, such as bulbs in glass jars, so that the children will be able to see the roots growing into the water and the flowers developing as the weeks go by.

CRAFT ACTIVITIES

PETER SHIELDS

You will need: cardboard shield shapes covered with paper and white emulsion (the sides of large cardboard boxes are ideal for making shields big enough for the children to wear); a copy of a St Peter's motif; pencils; paint; brushes; string or ribbon.

Chat about it

Talk to the children about the time when Jesus told Peter that he would be the rock on which Jesus would build his Church (Matthew 16:17–19). In this passage, Jesus tells Peter that he will be given the keys to the kingdom of heaven. It is for this reason that Peter is often depicted in religious art holding the keys of heaven, and the keys are his emblem. Talk about how Peter's faith was severely tested, and how Jesus forgave him for his lack of faith. Explain that we, too, can be forgiven, even when we lose faith or are too scared to own up to it. Faith can be like a shield because it helps us to deal with difficult situations by trusting God for the best answer.

Make it

Show the children Peter's emblem. Invite them to draw it on to their shields and then paint it or decorate it in some other way. Acrylic paint will give a good finish in a bright colour for this purpose. Finish the shields by attaching string or ribbon to form a handle at the back of each shield.

FAITH BOXES

You will need: small boxes with lids; PVA glue; items to decorate, such as glitter, sequins, beads, and so on; small pieces of paper; pens.

Chat about it

Discuss with the children how faith is something precious, which we keep safe in our hearts, minds and souls. Remind them that the Jewish people used to carry the Ten Commandments (representing the heart of their faith) with them wherever they went. They were also commanded to fasten the Mezuzah, a parchment scroll containing the law and placed inside a small box, to the doorposts of their houses and to their gates (Deuteronomy 11:20).

Tell the children that just because we can't see faith, it doesn't mean it isn't real. We carry faith round inside ourselves. A faith box can be a reminder that faith is real.

Make it

Give each child a small box (obtainable in craft shops or via the Internet). Invite each child to decorate his or her box, being careful to ensure that the lid will still go on (and come off). Ask them to make the box look as special as possible. When the boxes are finished, invite the children to write something they believe on a small piece of paper, fold it up and put it in their faith box.

ACORN BADGES

> **You will need:** thick card acorn shapes (see page 185); safety pins; sticky tape; pipe cleaners; light-coloured wool; paint; sponges; pens.

Chat about it

This activity is designed to help children think about how the seed of faith can grow. If your children's group has a name related to growing (for example, Acorns and Saplings), this activity will be particularly pertinent, because it will help the children to think about their identity as part of the group. You could adapt the idea to fit in with your own group's identity. Also, faith gives children an identity as part of God's family. Talk about how, with God's help, faith helps us to grow together.

Make it

Give each child an acorn shape. They may need help to attach the safety pin to the back with sticky tape, or you could have some badges ready prepared with pins fastened to the badge. Invite the children to use the sponges to paint the acorn. Add a pipe cleaner for the shoot (tape it to the back of the badge), and glue on a few strands of wool for the roots. Children could complete their badges either by adding their names to the front or by writing a short Bible phrase connected with faith, such as 'There are some things that people cannot do, but God can do anything' (Luke 18:27), or 'God loved the people of this world so much that he gave his only Son, so that everyone who has faith in him will have eternal life' (John 3:16), or 'Nothing in all creation can separate us from God's love for us in Christ Jesus our Lord!' (Romans 8:39).

PAPER CHAIN PEOPLE

You will need: paper such as newspaper or tissue paper for the chain; scissors; person template (see page 186) to draw round.

Chat about it

Talk about the fact that, as Christians, we are not alone. We are supported in faith by other Christians and must support others in our turn. When the children have opened out their concertinas to find a row of people, talk to them about the community of faith. Talk about who, for them, is part of that community.

Make it

Show the children how to fold the paper to make a concertina. You will need to adjust the width to match the width of your template. Draw round the person template, making sure that the hands and feet go right to the edge. Then cut out the person, making sure you don't cut round the hands and feet. Invite the children to make their own chain of people. Depending on the age of the children, some will need more help than others in folding and cutting.

WATCH IT GROW!

You will need: mustard and cress seeds; water; cotton wool or kitchen paper; containers (such as plastic trays or plates, or clean egg shells with the tops cut off); pens.

Chat about it

This activity links neatly with the Bible focus and is another illustration of how faith grows.

Make it

Provide the children with containers. Put the cotton wool or kitchen paper in the container and moisten it. Invite the children to sow their seeds. Tell them to keep their seeds somewhere warm and sunny, but not hot, and to look after them by keeping them moist. The children can watch as the tiny plants grow. (If they use egg shells as their containers, they will get the effect of a face, with cress as hair.)

COCKEREL FEATHER COLLAGE

You will need: cockerel shapes cut from card (see page 187); glue; feathers; googlie eyes or felt.

Chat about it

This activity links well with the story of Peter's denial and Jesus' subsequent forgiveness of him. While the children are working, talk about what Peter must have felt like when he betrayed his faith, what Jesus might have thought about it, and how it might have affected Peter's growth in faith for the rest of his life if Jesus hadn't put things right.

Make it

Invite the children to use the feathers to fill in the cockerel shape.

SHEEP-SHAPED BISCUITS

> **You will need**: sheep-shaped biscuit cutters; rolling pin; baking parchment; biscuit dough (see page 130 for recipe); access to hot oven.

Chat about it

This activity links with the follow-up to Peter's denial and Jesus' command to him to 'feed my lambs' (John 21:15). Talk about the story of the breakfast on the beach and the way that Jesus forgave Peter's lack of faith.

Make it

Give each child some of the biscuit dough and sheep-shaped biscuit cutters. Invite them to roll out the dough and then cut out sheep shapes. Put the biscuits on named pieces of baking parchment and bake in the oven. If you have kitchen facilities, this will be easy; if not, perhaps a friendly neighbour will be prepared to bake for you. If neither of these is possible, the children could take the dough home unbaked, with instructions on how to bake it at home.

As with any food activity, check whether any child has allergies.

If the biscuit dough you are using has egg in it, make sure they don't eat the raw dough. You will need hand-washing facilities (for before and after the activity) if you have no running water. A plastic washing-up bowl, water warmed in a kettle, some soap and towels would be fine.

GAMES

BREEZE BALL RACING

You will need: pre-cut circles of card (though older children could cut their own), with points marked or cut (see diagram overleaf); electric fan or a natural breeze; pens to write a message.

Chat about it

Talk to the children about faith and how you can tell it is there. As faith is invisible, it can be hard to tell if someone has faith or not. In this respect, it is a bit like the wind or air: you can't tell it is there unless it is blowing things around. Use a breeze ball to illustrate this point.

Play it

Invite the children to write a faith message or Bible verse, such as 'The Spirit is like the wind that blows wherever it wants to' (John 3:8) round the outside of their circle, on both sides. The children can decorate the message if they wish (and if you have time). Then show them how to bend the points of the triangles alternately one way, then the next, so that they have a spiky sort of ball. Place the balls on their edge in front of the fan or outside in a natural breeze. Turn on the fan and watch the balls roll in the breeze.

After a test run, use the balls for a race. Either use the fan or, if the children have enough puff, they could blow the balls across the floor to a designated finishing line.

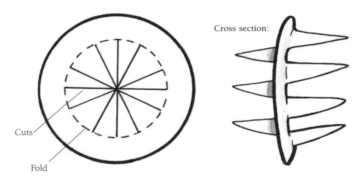

TAKE A PENCIL FOR A WALK

You will need: A3 paper; pencils.

Chat about it

Use this activity to talk about the way we don't always see the full picture. It is not always easy to know that what we're doing is what God wants us to do, so we have to have faith that he is there with us and that what we are doing is in line with his will.

Play it

Give each child a piece of paper and a pencil. Ask them to shut their eyes and take their pencils for a walk by drawing a long wiggly line on their paper. The children need to try to keep the pencil from straying off the edges of the paper, and to draw without lifting the pencil off the page. After 30 seconds (perhaps less), ask the children to stop drawing and open their eyes.

Each child then passes his or her paper to the person on their left, who looks at the new drawing in front of them and finds something, somewhere in the shapes, that could be made into a picture. They shade in the shape so that it looks like the object they have thought of. They could add details, such as eyes, if they wish.

The drawings are passed on again and the next child does the same. Keep going until everyone has had enough or the children receive their original drawing back again.

PRAYERS

WRITE-YOUR-OWN LITANY

> **You will need**: a copy of a psalm, such as Psalm 150, or other suitable litany; pens; sheets of paper; candles; candle lighters; fire precaution materials; bubble mixture and blowers.

Read a litany of praise to the children, such as Psalm 150, and talk about how it is written and how it might express someone's faith. Invite the children to write their own litanies. Older children might enjoy writing their own psalms and then contributing their best line to a group prayer. Younger children might prefer to be part of a group effort, with each child contributing one line. The resulting prayer could be said at the end of your session, perhaps with each child saying his or her own line. If children are reluctant to write, make sure an adult is available to write their ideas down for them.

You could develop the prayer by making up actions to express each line. Alternatively, you could try either blowing bubbles or lighting a candle after each line is said, to give time to think about each part of the prayer.

SAINTLY PRAYERS

> **You will need:** children's books about saints; candles and candle lighters; fire precaution materials; bubble mixture and blowers.

Use the books to help the children think about the lives of saints, or, if the children have some knowledge of saints, ask each child to think about their favourite saint and give a reason why they like that saint. Use these ideas to form a prayer thanking God for all the saints who have made the journey of faith before us.

If children are not so familiar with saints, ask them to think about the people in their lives who have helped (or are helping) them to get to know God. Make a prayer thanking God for all the people who show us the way to faith. A candle could be lit or bubbles blown for each person or saint mentioned.

KENNING PRAYERS

> **You will need:** small pieces of card; either a bowl or a picture or shape, such as a cross.

Talk to the children about the 'I am...' sayings of Jesus. (These sayings form the basis for a range of activities in the holiday programme starting on page 150.) Talk about how the sayings might be changed or developed into kennings to create different words for

God, such as 'flock-feeder', 'light-shiner', 'joy-maker' and so on.

If you need more inspiration, look at the chapter on 'I am' in *The Gospels Unplugged* by Lucy Moore (Barnabas, 2002).

Invite the children to make their own kennings and write them on the pieces of card. Use these kennings to make a prayer of praise. The children could read their kennings aloud, or they might prefer to stick them on to a picture or shape, or place them in a bowl as a prayer offering. The cards could be attached (temporarily) to the altar cloth if you have one.

Theme 3

PRAYER:
'PRAY IN THIS WAY...'

KEY BIBLE FOCUS: LUKE 11:1–10

Exploring prayer is a good way to help children understand how they can make and keep a relationship with God. Don't forget to remind the children that they can listen to God as well as talking to him.

BIBLE STORIES

The story of Jesus teaching the disciples how to pray is probably the obvious story to use here. As well as reading from a Bible version, it is worth considering other ways of exploring the story. The *Godly Play* version of the Lord's Prayer written by Sue Doggett works very well and will help to create a prayerful atmosphere. You will find the script and instructions in the 'Ideas' section of the Barnabas website, www.barnabasinchurches.org.uk. There is also a version of the story in Lucy Moore's book *The Lord's Prayer Unplugged* (Barnabas, 2004), which gives a comic view, with a serious point too.

If you want to supplement the Bible story, perhaps for older children who are already very familiar with it, you might read out George Herbert's poem 'Prayer', which could form part of a meditation and promote further discussion.

PRAYER

Prayer the Church's banquet, Angels' age,
God's breath in man returning to his birth,
The soul in paraphrase, heart in pilgrimage,
The Christian plummet sounding heaven and earth;

Engine against the Almighty, sinner's tower,
Reversed thunder, Christ-side-piercing spear,
The six-days world transposing in an hour,
A kind of tune, which all things hear and fear;

Softness, and peace, and joy, and love, and bliss,
Exalted Manna, gladness of the best,
Heaven in ordinary, man well dressed,
The Milky Way, the bird of Paradise,

Church-bells beyond the stars heard, the soul's blood,
The land of spices; something understood.

GEORGE HERBERT (1593–1633)

DISPLAYS FOR THE CHURCH

PATHWAY PRAYERS

You will need: coloured chalks; a hard paved area outside the church building; a camera.

Invite the children to write their own prayers and pictures on a convenient pathway outside your church building. If you have a suitable path between the gate and the church door, you might use that, but make sure you seek permission first from your minister.

As the children are creating their prayers and pictures, talk to them about their prayers and about why it might be appropriate for the path to the church to be paved with prayer.

Take photographs of the prayers to display on a board in the church after the event. This will be especially helpful if the rain washes the prayers away before the wider congregation sees them on their way to church. Remind the children that, even though the rain has washed the prayers away, God still hears them.

PRAYER SCRAPBOOK

You will need: good-quality scrapbook; Post-it notes; small pieces of paper.

Introduce the idea of a prayer scrapbook for the church. Explain that this will be on show in church so that everyone can see the prayers that the children have written. Tell the children that they can add prayers to the scrapbook whenever they wish. Make sure they know that other people will read their prayers and that the prayers need to be general. Say that anything they wish to be private, between them and God, shouldn't go into the book. Invite the children to write their own prayers as the first entries in the scrapbook. If younger children wish to draw a picture prayer instead, encourage them that God will understand their pictures in the same way that he understands the written prayers.

As well as their own prayers, the children may like to cut out pictures or printed prayers to paste into the scrapbook. They may also use a suitable item, such as a feather or a sticker, as a basis for a prayer.

COLOURING PRAYERS

You will need: published prayers printed out on plain paper with a border outline suitable for colouring in; colouring equipment (pencils, pens, or inks for older children).

Chat about it

Read the chosen prayers with the children and talk about what they mean.

Make it

Invite the children to decorate a prayer to make it look special. Allow 15 minutes for this activity, or perhaps 20 minutes for older children.

PRAYER PHONES

You will need: sturdy, good-quality plastic cups; buttonhole thread; sticky tape; an implement for making holes, such as a pair of compasses; Plasticine.

Chat about it

Talk to the children about how a homemade telephone works and explain that, when they come to make their phone, the string needs to be taut so that the vibrations from the voice can travel down it. Point out that praying to God is a bit different from using a telephone, because God is never out or engaged, and you don't need a special number or code to get through.

Make it

Make a hole in the bottom of each plastic cup in advance by placing a lump of Plasticine inside the cup and pushing the compasses' spike through the plastic. Cut the buttonhole thread into 2-metre lengths. Thread the buttonhole thread through the base of one cup and secure the end by tying a large knot in it. Fix the knotted end of the thread to the inside of the cup with sticky tape. Using the other end of the thread, repeat with a second cup, so that the two cups are connected by the thread.

Put the children into pairs. Ask each member of the pair to take hold of one of the cups and carefully stand apart so that the thread is taut but not overstrained. Show the children how to use the cups as a microphone or a speaker, by taking it in turns to speak into one cup while the other person holds their cup to their ear. Invite the children, in pairs, to use the telephones to talk to each other.

GAMES

PRAYER CODES

You will need: copies of invented codes; paper; pens or pencils.

Chat about it

Discuss with the children all the different ways of communicating, such as words, gestures, pictures and so on. Explain that we can use any of these ways to talk to God.

Play it

Using a combination of shapes and colours, ask the children to invent a code for the alphabet. For example, the letter 'E' might be represented by a blue triangle, the letter 'S' by a red circle, and so on. Alternatively, they could devise letter codes—for example, by shifting the letters of the alphabet along one (so that 'A' is represented by a letter 'B' and so on) or going backwards (so that 'A' is represented by a letter 'Z' and so on). When they have devised their codes, ask the children to write a simple prayer using the code. Invite the children to swap their prayer and the code they have used with someone else, so that they can work out what the other person's prayer says. You could play the game in teams (or pairs), with the winning team being the first to crack the code and recite the prayer.

SHIP AHOY

You will need: multiple copies of the different flags used for naval signals (see www.scoutingresources.org.uk/codes); string.

Chat about it

Chat about the fact that we can communicate by sight, even when we are not within listening distance. When we pray, we can use artefacts to focus our prayers, such as a candle, some pebbles, shells or feathers. However, God is always in listening distance, even when we don't use words.

Play it

Put the children into teams and have enough copies of each flag for the teams to be able to create a simple message with the letters. Retain a set for your own use. When the children have decided on their message, tell them to tie the flags along the string to make the message. The first team to complete their message and enable a leader to read it from a distance is the winning team.

Younger children might like to make their names as a string of flags.

SEMAPHORE PRAYERS

You will need: a list of semaphore signals (these can be found on www.scoutingresources.org.uk); paper; pens or pencils.

Chat about it

Talk to the children about the semaphore flag signalling system, which is based on the alphabet. Establish what the conventions are going to be for signalling the end of the message and providing gaps between words.

Play it

Place the children in two groups some distance apart (beyond comfortable talking distance) and give each group a copy of the semaphore code alphabet. If possible, the game can be played outside; if it is raining, you could use the church building. In their groups, invite the children to make up a simple prayer. As sending the signals will take some time, the prayer will need to be short; a 'thank you' or 'praise God' would be fine to begin with. One group then sends their prayer to the other group using the signals. The children in the group can take it in turns to signal one letter at a time, so that everyone has a chance to use the code. Sending will need to be slow enough for the receivers either to decipher as they go along or to write the code down to work out later. Swap round so that each group has a turn at being the prayer senders and the prayer receivers.

PRAYER WHISPERS

No equipment is required for this game.

Chat about it

Chat to the children about how important it is to listen to God as well as talk to him. Discuss in what form we might get an answer to our prayers. Often it is hard to hear and understand what God might be saying. The more we pray, the more comfortable we will be in God's company and the easier it will be to recognize it when he speaks to us. Explain that you are going to play a traditional game of Chinese Whispers to demonstrate the importance of listening as well as talking.

Play it

Put the children in a long line and ask the first child to make up a simple prayer. When ready, ask him or her to whisper the prayer to the next child, and so on down the line. When the prayer reaches the end of the line, ask the last child to say the prayer out loud. If it is correct, everyone can say 'Amen'; if not, find out what the prayer should have been and then say 'Amen' together.

You will need: paper; pens or pencils; compilation of everyday sounds; laptop computer (or MP3 player, such as an iPod, and speakers), or a tape recorder.

Chat about it

Talk about the gift of sound and all the wonderful and amazing sounds there are in the world. Explain that we often close our ears to the everyday sounds around us; because they are so familiar, we take them for granted. Point out that familiar sounds are part of the fabric of everyday life and thereby a symbol of God's care of us.

Play it

Prepare a compilation of household or everyday sounds that the children will all have heard, such as a running tap, boiling kettle, washing machine, ticking clock and so on. Preview sound effects can be downloaded free of charge from Internet sites such as www.sounddogs.com, or you could use a tape recorder to make your own. Make sure there is a mixture of obvious and more obscure sounds. Make a note of the sounds you have downloaded and in what order they occur. You will need either a laptop computer or an MP3 player and speakers to play the game in your venue.

When you are ready to play the game, give each child a pencil and paper. Play the sounds to them, repeating each sound twice, and ask them to write down what they think each one is.

Go through the sounds again, taking the children's ideas about what the sound could be, and reveal what they actually were. The child who gets the most sounds right is the winner.

TOUCH PRAYERS

Chat about it

Talk about the gift of touch and how God can communicate to us through the sense of touch. For example, holding a baby, feeling different textures in the natural world and holding hands are all reminders of how God reaches out to us with his love.

Play it

Arrange the children in two lines, with the children in each line standing one behind the other, so that each child is looking at the back of the child in front. Ask the person at the back of each line to think of a one- or two-word prayer (such as 'thank you', 'sorry' or 'please') and, using their finger, to 'write' their prayer word one letter at a time on the back of the person in front. They will need to press firmly enough for the front person to feel it, but not too roughly. The second person 'writes' the message on to the back of the person in front of them, and so on down the line. When the message gets to the end, the front person writes the prayer word on to a piece of paper. Compare it to the original message and see what has happened to it. The team that finishes first with the correct message is the winning team.

PRAYERS

EMAILS TO GOD

> **You will need:** e-shaped pieces of paper; pencils; pens.

Talk with the children about electronic methods of communication. Give each child an 'e' shaped piece of paper and writing materials. Invite them to write an email prayer to God. Talk about how, although prayer is an ancient art, it is not outdated or old-fashioned. We can talk to God about our lives today—about what is happening to our world and to us. We don't need to be distant and formal with God, but can talk to him in the same way as we might send an email to our closest friends. The emails can be added to the prayer scrapbook if you have one.

GRAFFITI WALL

> **You will need:** a very large piece of paper marked with brick shapes to look like a wall; masking tape or sticky tack; felt-tipped pens.

Fix the paper 'wall' to a suitable wall in your venue. Give out the felt-tipped pens and invite the children to write their prayers on the wall as graffiti. Alternatively, lay the paper wall on the floor and fix it to a wall after the children have completed their graffiti prayers. For a more permanent display, you could make your wall out of boxes instead.

PRAYING WITH OBJECTS

You will need: objects to evoke prayers relevant to the children, such as a model house to represent home, a book to represent school, a ring to represent the world outside our own lives, a teddy bear to represent other children, and so on.

Invite the children to sit in a circle, and show them the objects. Talk about what these things might mean to each of us. Explain that the objects will be passed round the circle one by one, and invite each child to pray silently in whatever way they like as they hold each object in turn.

THE LORD'S PRAYER WITH ACTIONS

No equipment is needed for this prayer activity.

Work through the Lord's Prayer with the children, talking about the meaning of each part. Then, with the children, have a go at inventing a way of praying it by using gestures for each line or phrase. Put the gestures together and pray the prayer through a few times.

WALK THE LORD'S PRAYER

Lucy Moore's book *The Lord's Prayer Unplugged* suggests excellent ideas for exploring the Lord's Prayer, including a way to walk the prayer by placing different objects at stations around your space, inviting everyone to walk round them and pray the relevant part of the prayer at each station.

Theme 4

MIRACLES:
WIND AND WAVES

KEY BIBLE FOCUS: MARK 4:35–41

The miracles of Jesus are an important part of the gospel message: the four Gospels record some 35 miracles in total. However, sometimes we are reluctant to tell the stories of Jesus' miracles to children, perhaps because we are wary of things that can't be explained. It is advisable to choose carefully which stories to tell and how to handle them in order to avoid presenting Jesus as a magician, but without the miracle stories we are in danger of misrepresenting the full picture of Jesus.

BIBLE STORIES

Stories of miracles that would be suitable to share with children include the storm on the lake (Mark 4:35–41), the wedding at Cana (John 2:1–10), Jairus' daughter (Luke 8:40–42 and 49–56), the centurion's servant (Luke 7:1–10), Jesus walks on water (Matthew 14:22–33), the feeding of the 5000 (Mark 6:30–44), the healing of the crippled man (Mark 2:1–12) and the raising of Lazarus (John 11:1–44).

Miracle stories often work well when told directly to the children without the aid of a book. In this way, it is easier to gauge how the children are responding and the storyteller can embellish parts of the story to spark the children's imaginations (for example, by describing the lake and the disciples' feelings throughout in the story of the stilling of the storm). With a little preparation and practice beforehand, most of the stories suggested above are easy to remember and retell in your own words.

DISPLAYS FOR THE CHURCH

The feeding of the 5000 lends itself to an ideal display for the church. You will need a large piece of paper—a length cut from a roll of lining paper would be ideal—brightly coloured fingerpaints or poster paints, distributed in small trays, and hand-washing equipment.

First of all, tell the children the story of the feeding of the 5000 (Mark 6:30–44). Ask them if they have ever seen such a large crowd of people. Explain that they are going to create a picture to demonstrate just how big a crowd it was. Show the children the paint and invite them to make fingerprints on the paper. This needs to be done carefully so that the prints can be counted: for example, it will be easiest if you instruct the children to place all ten digits simultaneously in the paint and then on to the paper. Try to get the different colours distributed evenly over the paper. The idea is to create 5000 fingerprints. If your group is very small, however, children could create 1000 prints and then imagine what five times as many would look like

If you have time, you might want to add bodies and draw faces on to the prints in the foreground. An image of two bread rolls and five small fishes displayed next to the finished picture would add to the impact.

CRAFT ACTIVITIES

BLOW PAINTING

You will need: good-quality thick paper (not too absorbent); drinking straws; runny poster paint in stormy colours; thicker white paint, spoons; pens; small brushes; sponges.

Chat about it

Chat about what it feels like to be caught in a thunderstorm, and then lead into telling the children the story of the storm on the lake (Mark 4:35–41).

Make it

Give each child a piece of paper and invite them to put small pools of paint on to it using the teaspoons. Show them how they can blow through the straw to disperse the paint. Ask them to fill the paper and blend their colours to make an interesting stormy design. When the paint is dry, the children could paint a small boat (or boats) on their stormy sea, and perhaps add some thicker white paint, using a sponge, to make foamy waves.

SPILLAGE PAINTING

You will need: large sheets of good-quality paper; cold tea (without milk) or blackcurrant juice; plastic cups; drawing pencils.

Chat about it

Tell the children the story of the wedding at Cana (John 2:1–10) and explain that this was the first miracle Jesus performed. The Bible tells us that this miracle showed people who Jesus really was and that his closest friends put their faith in him. John tells us that the stone jars were filled to the top, and this image is often seen to symbolize God's love spilling over in Jesus.

Make it

Give each child a large sheet of good-quality paper. Pour a little tea or blackcurrant juice into plastic cups. Show the children how to pour a very small amount on to their pieces of paper and then tilt the paper so that the liquid runs in random lines over it. Look at the patterns the children have made and talk about what they look like. Invite the children to turn their spillages into drawings using their pencils. The pictures can be related to the story by creating something to remind them of the wedding or the stone jars. Alternatively, the children can just use their imaginations to create an abstract picture.

CHROMATOGRAPHY

You will need: filter papers; water; pipette; pens.

Chat about it

Talk about how some things can look like miracles even though they are not. For example, many things in science might seem to be miracles, but they can be explained. After the activity, chat about the different colours that make up what looks like a single colour.

Make it

Give the children a piece of filter paper each and ask them to draw a dot (it needs to be a sizeable one, not just a full stop size) of colour in the centre. Invite them then, very carefully, to use the pipette to drip water slowly on to the centre of the dot, just a drop at a time. As the water spreads over the paper, it will take some of the pigments with it. Because different pigments will be dispersed at different rates, the effect is (often) several rings of different colours around the initial dot from the pen. Experiment beforehand to find the best pens to use: black ones often give the most spectacular results. What looks like black ink can contain several different colours.

FLAT-ROOFED HOUSES

You will need: illustrations of flat-roofed houses; cardboard boxes; poster paint; paintbrushes; strips of medium-weight card; sticky tape; scissors.

Chat about it

Tell the children the story of the healing of the crippled man (Mark 2:1–12). Talk about how the man's friends might have managed to let him down through the roof on his bed, and look at some pictures of biblical houses. Talk about how houses at this time were constructed, so that it was not difficult to make such a hole in the roof.

Make it

Invite the children to use the boxes to make their own models of biblical houses. Remember to include the steps up the outside of the house on to the flat roof. You could either make one large house with the whole group (using a large cardboard box), or each child could make his or her own house (using smaller boxes).

GAMES

MIRACLES / NOT MIRACLES

You will need: the list of situations suggested on page 62.

Chat about it

Talk about the miracles of Jesus, especially those that the children have explored in the storytelling and crafts. Talk about the people who witnessed Jesus' miracles. Look at some of the miracles in the Bible and find out how people reacted to what they saw. Read 1 John 1:1–4 to the children and explain that the Gospel writers (Matthew, Mark, Luke and John) were inspired to write down what they had seen and heard about Jesus, because they knew that it was too important to be lost. It is their accounts that have given us the Gospels we know today.

Play it

Have the children congregate in one area of your hall or church building. Designate one area 'miracle' and a different area 'not miracle'. Explain that they have to decide whether or not the situations or events you call out are miracles. If they think the situation or event is a miracle, they move to the area designated as 'miracle'. If they don't think it is a miracle, they move to the area designated as 'not miracle'.

Call out some of the examples below and then bring the children together to discuss how they decided which was which. Is there a way to determine whether something is or isn't a miracle? Finish with some more examples and more discussion if required or desired.

Include examples of biblical and non-biblical stories, such as the suggestions below, but mix them up so that there is no pattern to the situations or events as you call them out.

★ Jesus turning water into wine (the wedding at Cana)
★ Jesus walking on the water
★ Jesus bringing Jairus' daughter back to life
★ Jesus calming the storm
★ Moses' parting of the Red Sea
★ Noah and the animals surviving the flood
★ Jonah living inside the whale for three days
★ Daniel surviving a night in the lions' den
★ Contemporary stories of healing (for example, at Lourdes)
★ Someone walking on the moon
★ Someone performing a magic trick
★ Someone having a successful heart transplant
★ Someone using the Internet or sending an email
★ Someone using a mobile phone
★ A gripping survival story
★ Weather phenomena such as rainbows

WOUNDS AND BANDAGES

You will need: fake wounds, such as those used by first aiders (optional); bandages; a skilled first aider.

Chat about it

Talk about how Jesus healed people. Chat about the different sorts of people he helped and how he helped them. In biblical times, outward illness or injury was seen as a sign of inward wrongdoing. Talk about what that would mean for the people Jesus healed.

Play it

If you know someone who is an experienced first aider, they may be able to create (fake) wounds and then treat them. The children (generally) will be fascinated to try this out! The fake wounds add a bit of spice but, if you can't manage to make fake wounds, just use bandages.

Ask the first aider to demonstrate how to apply a bandage to a wound. Then put the children into pairs and give each pair a bandage. If you are using fake wounds, ask a leader to apply a fake wound to one child in each pair. If you are just using bandages, this is fine, too. The other child now has to apply the bandage in the way demonstrated by the first aider. Award points for the best-applied bandage.

You could expand this into a team game. Give each team a supply of bandages and ask a volunteer from each team to sit at the far end of the playing space. The team members then have to take turns to run down the course and apply a bandage to the volunteer as commanded by the leader (for example, a bandage for a broken wrist, a broken arm, a damaged knee, or a bump on the head). The team with the best-bandaged volunteer is the winning team.

THE CENTURION'S SERVANT

> **You will need:** fresh bread; a table; some plates; a bread machine (optional); a candle; matches or a candle lighter; fire precaution materials; a candle extinguisher.

Lay the table properly with cloth and plates. Place the candle in the middle of the table. If you have a bread machine, the smell, texture and taste of freshly cooked bread is always very evocative. Light the candle.

Talk about the story of the centurion's servant (Luke 7:1–10) and remind the children that words based on those used by the centurion ('I am certainly not worthy to come to you. Just say the word, and my servant will get well': v. 7) are sometimes used at a service of Holy Communion. Discuss with the children what these words mean. Remind them that the centurion was not a member of the Jewish nation, but was part of the occupying Roman forces in Jesus' time.

Say a prayer over the bread to ask for God's blessing and then break and share the bread among the children. Be as formal or informal as you like. Perhaps the children could take turns to thank God for a gift he has given them before the bread is broken, or after it is shared and before it is eaten.

HEALING

Lots of Jesus' miracles involved healing. Talk about some of them to the children, and bring out the fact that it is not just physical injuries or illness that might need to be healed, but also mental scars and spiritual difficulties. Then invite the children to think of people who need God's healing touch, whether in body or spirit. You could either incorporate their ideas into a prayer or ask them to draw a picture or write the names of the people they wish to pray for on pieces of paper. The papers could be pinned to a strip of bandage to be hung up in church.

Remember to include people who try to help others in the healing process, such as doctors, nurses, ministers in the church, therapists and so on. You might want to include a prayer for the work of an organization such as the Red Cross (these prayers could be stuck on to a large red cross).

Theme 5

PARABLES:
ARE YOU SITTING COMFORTABLY?

KEY BIBLE FOCUS: MARK 4:10–11

The Bible tells us that Jesus taught many things using stories (Matthew 13:3; Mark 4:2). His parables were stories designed to make people think and work out the meaning for themselves. For those who desire to find out more about Jesus, his parables are an excellent way to deepen understanding of his teaching.

BIBLE STORIES

The Synoptic Gospels (Matthew, Mark and Luke) are full of parables, any of which is ideal to use with children. Those found only in Matthew's Gospel include:

* Weeds among wheat (Matthew 13:24–30)
* A hidden treasure (13:44)
* A valuable pearl (13:45–46)
* A fishing net (13:47–50)
* New and old treasure (13:52)
* The official who refused to forgive (18:21–35)
* Ten girls (25:1–13)

Parables found only in Luke's Gospel include:

* ☆ The good Samaritan (Luke 10:25–37)
* ☆ A friend at midnight (11:5–10)
* ☆ A rich fool (12:13–21)
* ☆ A fig tree (13:6–9)
* ☆ A lost coin (15:8–10)
* ☆ Two sons (15:11–32)
* ☆ A dishonest manager (16:1–13)
* ☆ Lazarus and the rich man (16:19–31)
* ☆ A widow and a judge (18:1–8)
* ☆ A Pharisee and a tax collector (18:9–14)

Parables found in more than one Gospel include:

* ☆ A farmer (Matthew 13:1–9; Mark 4:1–9; Luke 8:4–8)
* ☆ A rich young man (Matthew 19:16–24; Mark 10:17–31; Luke 18:18–30)
* ☆ A mustard seed and yeast (Matthew 13:31–33; Mark 4:30–32; Luke 13:18–21)
* ☆ Tenants in a vineyard (Matthew 21:33–46; Mark 12:1–12; Luke 20:9–19)
* ☆ A lost sheep (Matthew 18:10–14; Luke 15:3–7)
* ☆ The great banquet (Matthew 22:1–14; Luke 14:15–24)
* ☆ Two builders (Matthew 7:24–27; Luke 6:47–49)

There are many creative ways to tell parables. First of all, you can simply tell the story using your own words, or using a Bible such as the Contemporary English Version (CEV), or a children's Bible such as *The Barnabas Children's Bible* (Barnabas, 2007). Alternatively, you could tell the story using visual aids such as model figures and other artefacts, or with audience participation by giving the children actions or words to say at certain trigger points in the story. Finally, you could use role play, drama, dance or mime to act out the story with the children.

Choose a parable from the list above, or any other parable you wish to explore with the children. Tell the story using any of the suggested methods. Now work out a way that the story could be told as a performance piece. Practise the piece with the children, adding actions as appropriate. Make sure all the children are included in non-speaking roles, but also identify children who would like to have a speaking role and encourage them to participate in this way.

Practise the performance parable a few times and then, when everyone is ready, arrange to take it into the church and perform it to the congregation during a set service. Alternatively, invite friends and family of the children and the wider church community to your group for the performance. Advertise the performance beforehand and have someone write a piece for your church newsletter afterwards. See *The Gospels Unplugged* by Lucy Moore (Barnabas, 2002), which contains a performance poem based on the parable of the farmer.

CRAFT ACTIVITIES

PARABLE FIGURES

You will need: modelling equipment such as Plasticine, playdough or foil.

Chat about it

Tell the children the parable using one of the methods outlined above and then explore the characters in the story with the children. Decide which characters are involved and what their role is. The good Samaritan (Luke 10:25–37) is an example of a parable that works well for this activity.

Make it

Invite each child to make a model of one of the figures that appear in the story. Once the models are ready, put them on a cloth or stage area and tell or retell the parable, allowing the children to move the figures around as the story progresses. You could do this a couple of times to give the children time to try out the activity and decide how best to move the characters.

PARABLE PLATE FACES

You will need: whole paper plates; paints; brushes; some paper plates cut in half; sticky tape; short garden canes.

Chat about it

Choose a parable with plenty of characters, such as the story of the ten girls (Matthew 25:1–13) or the great banquet (22:1–14). Begin by telling the story to the children, then ask them to think about the characters in the story and whether they are happy or sad. Are they always happy? Always sad? Or do their feelings change as the story progresses?

Make it

Give each child a whole and a half plate. Use the sticky tape to fix the half paper plate over the whole one so as to form a hinge. Invite the children to paint or draw a face on the plate so that when the half-plate is down, the face is sad, but when it is lifted up, the face is happy. If you feel adventurous, you could make a device to move the flap (string threaded through a hole on the hinge and another at the top of the whole plate) or to keep it in place when it is up (such as stick-on Velcro).

Tape the plate face to a short garden cane and retell the parable you are using so that the children can show the reactions of the characters (or their own reactions) to the events.

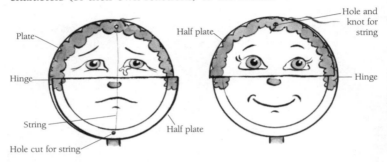

FRIENDSHIP STRINGS

You will need: fine cord; wool or embroidery thread; patience.

Chat about it

Explain to the children that some parables are about the way we treat other people and the sort of relationships we have with them, such as the parable of the friend at midnight (Luke 11:5–10) or the good Samaritan (Luke 10:25–37). Tell the children that you are going to be making friendship strings or bracelets for them to give to each other (or to people outside your group). Making friendship bracelets gives plenty of time for you and the children to talk about the story, and about how we should treat not just friends but also strangers (and even people we may not like very much).

Make it

The instructions below demonstrate one way to make braids, but you could use any other method you know.

> **You will need:** three strands of thread about 75cm long. Using three different colours will give a more interesting effect.

Tie the threads together a little way down from one end and tape or tie the ends to a solid object. Loop the left-hand thread (X) over the middle one, up and underneath it, and pull through towards the right (see the diagram below). Pull tight and repeat, knotting the same strands in the same pattern. Strand X will now be in the middle. Now loop the new middle strand (X) over the right-hand strand (Z), up and underneath it and through towards the right. Pull tight and repeat with the same strands. Strand X should now be at the right and strand Y on the left. Start again from the left, looping strand Y over and under the middle strand (Z) twice, then over and under the right-hand strand (X) twice, pulling each knot tight as you go. Continue until you have made a braid of the required length.

SPROUTING SEED BADGES

> **You will need:** thick card cut into the shape of seeds; safety pins; sturdy sticky tape such as insulation tape; pipe cleaners; light-coloured wool; poster paint; sponges; pens.

Chat about it

Choose a parable that features seeds, such as the story about the farmer (Matthew 13:1–9; Mark 4:1–9; Luke 8:4–8) or the mustard seed (Matthew 13:31–32; Mark 4:30–32; Luke 13:18–19). Tell the story to the children, using one of the methods suggested on page 67.

Make it

Give each child a seed shape to colour in by applying paint with a sponge. When the paint is dry, add a pipe cleaner for the shoot and a few strands of wool for the roots. Tape a safety pin to the back of the badge (younger children will need adult help). Children can then write their names on the front of the badge.

LOST SHEEP

> **You will need:** cardboard tubes; cotton wool; glue; black felt or card cut in the shape of sheep faces and feet; googlie eyes.

Chat about it

Tell the children the parable of the lost sheep (Luke 15:1–7), using one of the methods suggested on page 67. Ask the children if any of them have ever been lost. What did it feel like? What did it feel like to be found again? Discuss ways in which the children can keep themselves safe so that they don't get lost, but also talk about 'lost and found' games that we can play, such as Peek-a-boo with babies or Hide-and-seek with our friends.

This is a good activity to go with the lost sheep parable, particularly for younger children.

Make it

Cut along the length of each cardboard tube and then cut a semicircle out of each side of the cut edge. This will leave you with the rounded back of a sheep and four legs, which can be eased out so the cardboard sheep can stand up. Invite the children to cover the sheep with cotton wool fleeces, stick on face shapes and feet cut from black felt or card, and add the googlie eyes.

GAMES

FLOUR CONSTRUCTION

You will need: plenty of flour; water; container (such as a seed tray or sand tray); materials for construction, such as lolly sticks, tape, card, matchboxes, and so on.

Chat about it

Tell the children the parable of the two builders (Matthew 7:24–27) using one of the suggested methods on page 67. Talk about what the parable means in terms of our having strong foundations and the importance of listening to God and obeying what he teaches us.

Play it

Invite the children to test what happens when you build on materials that are not strong enough to take the structure. Give out the building materials and allow the children to make some buildings. Put flour in the container, place the completed buildings on the flour and add water (not too quickly). You may need to set up a current by gently tilting the tray for best effect. Watch to see what happens. Whose building lasts the longest?

BALANCING ACT

You will need: a container for flour (such as a seed tray or sand box); a mound of dry flour; spoons; a coin.

Chat about it

This game follows on from the previous one. Expand the teaching about the parable of the two builders (Matthew 7:24–27) by talking about what might happen if someone were to undermine our faith in God or our determination to follow Jesus.

Play it

Make a large mound of flour in the centre of the container and place a coin on top of the mound. Give each child a spoon. Invite the children, one at a time, to take one spoonful of the flour away from the mound. The object of the game is to balance the coin on a column of flour for as long as possible. The person whose spoonful topples the mound loses. Play the game until you have an overall winner. You could play the game with suitable sweets rather than a coin: the winner could then eat the sweet.

WHAT SHOULD I DO?

> **You will need:** a suitable parable about a dilemma, such as the good Samaritan (Luke 10:25–37), the dishonest manager (Luke 16:1–13), the official who refused to forgive (Matthew 18:21–35), or the two sons (Luke 15:11–32).

Chat about it

Tell the children the parable story until you get to the dilemma. Stop there and discuss what the options are. With some parables, such as the good Samaritan, you will need to make sure the children understand the reasons why the first two passers-by decided not to help.

Play it

Choose one child to be the person who has to decide the best thing to do in the situation created in the parable. Ask the rest of the children to line up in two lines. Designate one line as those in favour and the other as those against. The child who has to make the decision then walks between the two lines (not too quickly) while the children in the two lines give their advice. Make sure the children in each line understand what sort of advice they should be giving. For example, if the decision maker represents the priest in the good Samaritan story, the line on the left might be in favour of him stopping to help, while those on the right are against, encouraging him instead to hurry on to his duties at the temple. The idea is that the children in the lines are the promptings of conscience for the person having to make the decision.

WRITE A PARABLE

You will need: paper; writing implements.

Chat about it

This activity is suitable for use with older children. Select a few of the shorter parables, such as the lost coin (Luke 15:8–10) or the two builders (Matthew 7:24–27), and invite the children to read them and explore how the meaning is hidden in the story. Have a discussion about the way a parable works. Remind them that the story needs to be based on situations people will understand, but should illustrate something about the nature of God or our relationship with him.

Play it

After the discussion, invite the children to write their own parable or draw a parable using storyboard frames and speech bubbles.

EYE OF THE NEEDLE

You will need: a Bible; a darning needle; props that denote royalty, such as a crown, sceptre, orb, fake jewels, and so on.

Chat about it

Read the story of the rich young man (Matthew 19:16–24) using one of the suggested storytelling methods on page 67. Show the children a darning needle and ask, 'Could a camel get though that?'

Then explain that the eye of the needle was the name of a gateway through the city walls of Jerusalem. Show the children a picture of a city gate (you should be able to find a picture on the Internet). Discuss with the children what they think the story means.

Play it

Split the group into two teams. Choose a volunteer from each team to stand at the opposite end of the playing area. Share out the props so that each team has the same number of items. In their teams, the children then take turns to pick up an item one at a time, run to their team player at the opposite end, hand them the item, run back to the team and tag the next person. The game continues until the volunteer is overloaded with items and has no spare hands to hold anything else.

When the teams have finished, stop the game and discuss whether we might like this person better now that they are so 'rich and powerful'. Does having a lot of things affect—or should it affect—who we are? Restart the game. This time, the team members have to take it in turns to run to the volunteer and shake hands with him or her, then run back and tag the next player and so on. Can the volunteer shake hands without dropping everything? The team whose volunteer manages to shake hands while holding on to the most items is the *losing* team—but don't let the children know that the team that *drops* most items is the winning team until after the game is over.

After the game, explain that sometimes we have to let go of things that we have, so that we can receive something more valuable. Even members of the royal family are just people when they are with their friends. Being friends with someone involves sharing. We can't be a true friend if we try to keep everything to ourselves. Finish by talking about how this affects the way we relate to God. It doesn't matter what we have; it's who we are that counts. God sees the person underneath all the wealth and power. If we want to be friends with God, we must be prepared to share all the good things he has given us with others.

You will need: pictures of the objects you will be hunting (or the objects themselves).

Chat about it

If you haven't already done so, tell the children a 'lost and found' parable (such as those in Luke 15), using one of the storytelling methods suggested on page 67. Talk about what it is like to look for something or someone who is lost. What would it feel like to lose something very valuable or very precious? Have any of the children ever lost anything that meant a lot to them, and then found it again? What did it feel like to lose that thing, and to find it?

Play it

Before the children arrive, hide your chosen pictures or objects around the meeting venue. Make sure that they are hidden well enough for the children not to spot them as soon as they arrive, but not so well that they can't find them when you come to play the game. You will also need to remember how many pictures or objects are hidden (100 might be too many!). Set the children to find all the items. If you use this game before a refreshment break, you can mirror the celebration in the parable with a drink and biscuit as a reward for finding all the missing items.

PRAYERS

EVERYDAY LIFE PRAYERS

If there is someone appropriate whom you could invite to talk to the children, you might like to welcome them to the group as a guest. For example, perhaps a farmer could talk about sowing seed and growing crops, a member of the Samaritans could talk about their work, or a respected local builder could talk about how to build houses so that they don't fall down.

Use their talk as a springboard into reflection about how Jesus taught stories about everyday life and how those stories contained truths about God. Finish by thanking God for all the ways that he communicates his love for us by his provision in everyday life.

FRIENDSHIP PRAYERS

Talk about what it means to be a true friend, like the person who helped in the story of the good Samaritan (Luke 10:25–37). Give out some writing materials and invite the children to write or draw prayers thanking God for friends and asking for his help to be a good friend to others. If you have made a prayer scrapbook (see page 46), you could add these prayers to it. The children might enjoy writing their prayers on shaped pieces of paper, such as hearts or stars.

When the children have finished writing or drawing their prayers, arrange the group in a circle. Pray together silently, or with a leader speaking, or each person in the circle taking a turn. The method you choose will depend on your group.

You will need: packets of seeds; a patch of prepared ground or a pot with compost.

Use seeds as an inspiration for prayer and an illustration of how we grow with God through listening and learning about him. Perhaps you could use wild flower seeds to cast over a suitable patch of ground, or plant larger seeds such as nasturtiums in pots, praying while you do it. Make sure you look after the seedlings. The sight of the plants growing will remind you for the rest of the year about how we grow with God.

Theme 6

BLESSINGS:
RECIPES FOR LIFE

KEY BIBLE FOCUS: MATTHEW 5:1–12

Although a lot we can learn about Jesus' teaching is contained in the stories he told and the accounts of what he did, it is also interesting to look at the teaching he delivered by just speaking to the crowds. In Matthew 5:1—7:29 we find some of Jesus' key teaching about forgiveness, love, and learning not to worry. This section of Matthew's Gospel is often known as the Sermon on the Mount, and the first twelve verses are called the Beatitudes.

BIBLE STORIES

There are a number of short Bible passages for you to use with this theme, depending on the area of teaching you want to emphasize. To gain an overview of the teaching, you could have a few verses to tell the children when they come to each activity, or pepper the session with some well-chosen key verses, rather than having a ten-minute story time on the teaching in the Sermon on the Mount itself.

Topics you could look at include:

★ Salt and light (Matthew 5:13–16; key verse: 16)
★ Forgiveness (5:38–42; key verse: 39)

* Love (5:43–48; key verse: 44)
* Giving (6:1–4; key verses: 3–4)
* Treasure: (6:19–21; key verse: 21)
* Worry (6:25–34; key verse: 30)
* Judging others (7:1–6; key verse: 1)
* Asking (7:7–12; key verse: 7)

DISPLAYS FOR THE CHURCH

Tell the children the story of Jesus' teaching about worry (Matthew 6:25–34). Talk about the things in the story that Jesus uses to show God's love and care for us. Talk about the things we worry about and what we can do to help ourselves not to worry. Put together the following banner to display in the church.

TESSELLATING BIRDS

You will need: lots of tessellating bird shapes (see page 188 for template); felt-tipped pens or pencils in bright colours; pens for writing; a large piece of black card or board; PVA glue.

Give each child a tessellating bird shape and ask them to colour it as they please. When they have finished colouring the bird shape, ask them to write on it something about Jesus' teaching in the story. The children could write something in their own words or write a Bible verse, such as the key verse suggested above. Glue each completed bird on to a large piece of black card for display.

DOOR POSTER

You will need: two large pieces of card; paper; drawing materials.

Prepare the card in advance. One piece will form the backing; the other will have doorways cut in it, one for each child in your group. (The size of the doorways will depend on the size of the card and the number of children.) On the doorway sheet, mark out where the doors will be and their shapes (they could be double or single doors). Once their positions are marked, cut round the opening edges and fold to make the hinges. Next, using the door sheet as a template, mark the corresponding position of each door on the backing sheet. Make sure the sizes, shapes and locations are clearly marked. When the two sheets are finally put together, you will have an Advent calendar effect. Draw the doorways also (at the same size) on separate pieces of paper, one doorway on each.

Start by talking to the children about Jesus' teaching in Matthew 7:7–12. Talk about the images that Jesus uses in the story and how the images help us to remember that God is ready to give us good things when we ask for them. Talk about what those good things might be. Talk about the things we need that are good for us, and the things we want that aren't necessarily good for us.

When you are ready to start the activity, give each child a piece of paper with one of the door openings marked on it. Invite them to create a scene that might be seen through an inviting doorway, such as a garden, a spectacular view, a wonderful room or anything else they choose. When the scenes are complete, they can be stuck in the appropriate places (already marked) on the backing sheet.

The children can then decorate the outside of the doors in whatever way they wish. For example, they might want big, heavy church-type doors, panelled doors, garage doors, French windows, prison doors and so on. Then stick the card with the doors cut into it on top of the backing sheet so that the children's scenes appear when the doors are opened. To finish the display, the children could write above the doors some of the phrases they particularly like from Jesus' teaching.

CRAFT ACTIVITIES

DECORATING FLOWER POTS

You will need: white emulsion paint; terracotta flower pots; acrylic paint; brushes; water.

Chat about it

Tell the story of Jesus' teaching on worrying about what we wear (Matthew 6:27–30). Talk about Jesus' use of the image of wild flowers to help us understand that we don't need to worry about the clothes we wear. How does his teaching sit with the culture of expensive designer clothing and ever-changing fashion trends?

Make it

You will need to prepare the flower pots in advance by painting them with white emulsion, which gives a better base for the children to apply their paint and will also give brighter colours.

Give everyone a flower pot and encourage the children to decorate their pot as they choose, using the acrylic paints. If the children will be planting the pots later in the session, discourage them from overloading the pots with too much paint, by pointing out that they will need time to dry. Although acrylic paint does dry quickly, it will take longer to dry if the paint is too thick.

You will need: A4 card folded to make double doors (see diagram); pens, pencils, wax crayons, and so on.

Chat about it

Talk to the children about Jesus' teaching on the way we should treat each other (Matthew 5:43–48; 7:12). Chat about how hard it is to like people who treat us badly. What can we do to improve the situation? Link the discussion to Jesus' teaching about forgiving each other (Matthew 5:38–42). As part of the discussion, make the point that bullying is never acceptable and that the children should always talk to a trusted adult if they are subjected to bullying. Talk about the things we could do to show each other that we care.

Make it

Have an example card ready to show the children. Explain that they will be making their own doorway, opening on to a scene that, for them, conveys a message about caring for each other. Invite the children to use the drawing materials to decorate the inside of the card with the scene of their choice. It could be an interior or an outside scene. They then need to decorate the outside of the card to look like doors, once again choosing their own colours and design. Inside the doors, they could write a message to someone they would like to give the card to, as a sign that they would welcome the opportunity to be friends with that person.

PLANTING WILD FLOWERS

You will need: terracotta flower pots (if the children have already decorated some, use these, otherwise plain ones will be fine); compost; a large seed tray to contain the compost; a little water; wild flower seeds.

Chat about it

If you are using this activity in conjunction with the flower pot painting to explore Jesus' teaching about worrying over what we wear, simply help the children to fill their pots with compost, moisten the compost a little, then invite the children to sow the seeds on the top.

Alternatively, tell the story of Jesus' teaching in Matthew 6:27–30 and follow it up with a discussion as suggested above.

Make it

If you have a patch of land outside your meeting room, such as a churchyard, which would benefit from some wild flowers, you could sow the seeds there, either in addition to or instead of using flower pots (making sure you have permission, of course). The children will then be able to enjoy at their leisure the plants and flowers that grow from the seeds.

BLESSING BOXES

You will need: small boxes with lids; glue; items to decorate the boxes, such as fake jewels, glitter, sequins, beads, and so on; small pieces of paper; pens.

Chat about it

Talk to the children about their favourite part of Jesus' teaching that they have heard so far. Discuss why they like that particular verse or section, and why it is valuable to them. If they can identify a favourite verse, see if they can have a go at memorizing it. Say that, to help them remember the verse, they are going to make a box to put it in.

Make it

Give each child a small box (obtainable in craft shops or via the Internet). Invite them to decorate their box, being careful to make sure the lid will still go on (and come off). Ask them to make the box look as special as they can. When the boxes are finished, invite the children to write out their favourite verse, fold it up and put it in their box. If they need to remind themselves about the verse, they know where they can find it easily.

FLOWER PAINTING

You will need: some good fresh flowers in an attractive vase; good-quality cartridge paper; pastels; watercolour pencils; some botanical art prints.

Chat about it

Chat about all the beautiful things God has given for us to enjoy. Talk about the things that show us how much God cares for our world and especially for us.

Make it

Look at the flowers with the children. Talk about what the children can see and encourage them to look really carefully at the shapes and colours. Show some botanical prints and talk about how detailed they are. Look at the flowers again. Give the children the materials and invite them to make the best pictures they can of the flowers. The children can use whichever materials they are most comfortable with, or they might want to try out both pencils and pastels.

GARDEN COLLAGE

You will need: stiff paper or thin card; PVA glue and spreaders; collage materials, such as cotton wool, foil, tissue, crêpe, magazine pictures, string, wool, twine, fabric, and so on.

Chat about it

Talk about Jesus' teaching on worrying about having something to eat. Chat about all the good things that God supplies for us to eat. Talk about the way that God looks after living creatures by supplying food and shelter for them. What can we do to help? What does this teaching say about the way we approach life? As they are working on the activity, talk with the children about how much God cares for his creation—including us.

Make it

Allow the children to create their own idea of a garden, using collage. They could incorporate flower beds, ponds, animals, fish, vegetables, soil, washing lines, fences, and so on. Encourage the children to take care to make as lovely a garden as they can. Depending on the children you have, they could either construct individual gardens or make a large one for display in church.

GAMES

WHAT'S THE WORD?

You will need: cards showing pictures of everyday actions together with a list of prohibited words.

Chat about it

Talk about the way that Jesus uses images to help us understand his teaching. Look at some of the images he uses to illustrate the point, such as salt and light, birds and flowers, doors, stones and snakes. Lead into thinking about the way we use words and images to communicate.

Play it

The children take turns to choose a card. They then need to explain how to do the action shown on the card, but without using the prohibited words. For example, they might need to explain how to do the washing up without mentioning the words 'washing', 'dishes', 'plates', 'liquid', or 'water'; or they might be asked to explain how to clean their teeth without saying 'teeth', 'brush' or 'toothpaste'. The other children have to guess what is being explained.

You might also challenge the children to give their explanations without making any hand gestures. This is quite difficult, particularly when trying to explain an action like throwing or catching a ball.

RECIPE FOR A GOOD LIFE

You will need: large sheets of paper; pens.

Chat about it

Read Matthew 5:1–12 to the children and talk about what Jesus' teaching in these verses means. Explain that God's blessings in these verses are like a recipe for a good life: the kind of person we must be to be blessed by God. Talk about the children's thoughts on what is necessary for us to live a good life.

Play it

Split the children into teams, with three or four children in each team. Have a leader with each group of children. In their teams, the children have to come up with a recipe for the things that are necessary for us to live a good life. They can put their suggestions together to give a list of ingredients (including quantities) and how they should be mixed. (An example might be, 'Take a handful of love and mix in a bowl with a good spoonful of prayer. Season with compassion and bake in a low oven for a lifetime.') Each team can share their recipe with the rest of the children. You could award a prize to the team with the best recipe for life.

You might publish the children's recipes in your church magazine, or you could leave the recipes on display for everyone to read.

WRITE-YOUR-OWN BLESSINGS

You will need: Bible; paper; pens.

Chat about it

This game would be more suited to older children. Read Matthew 5:1–12 and talk with the children about what the verses mean. Ask them what sort of words Jesus might have used if he had been giving this teaching today. Put the children into groups, with three or four children in each, and allocate an adult leader to each group. In their groups, ask the children to write some alternative blessings that would be suitable for people to hear today. When they are ready, ask them to share their suggestions with the rest of the children. If the children have made teaching boxes, they could keep their write-your-own blessings in their boxes.

PRAYERS

PRAYING WITH OBJECTS

Use different objects to stimulate prayer. If you have been concentrating on birds or flowers, you might use a feather or a petal. Similarly, you could use some salt and a tealight candle, or some bread and fish shapes cut out of holographic paper. Invite the children to look really closely at their objects. If you have magnifying glasses or a microscope, you could use them. Marvel at the wonder of creation and Creator and give thanks for the wonderful things he has made for us to enjoy.

Think about all the teaching contained in Matthew 5:1—7:29 and use it as a stimulus for prayer. Think about all the people who have helped us to a better understanding of God. The children might wish to name them and give thanks for them. Think also about the people whom we might bring nearer to God by what we say or do, or just who we are. Ask for help to be the people God wants us to be.

The children could write their own prayers, or you might wish to find appropriate prayers in a book.

Theme 7

FORGIVENESS:
SEVENTY TIMES SEVEN

KEY BIBLE FOCUS: MATTHEW 18:21–35

Forgiveness is a major theme in the Gospels: God's forgiveness of us, and ours of other people. Forgiveness of sins is often a precursor to healing miracles, too. Teaching about forgiveness is of prime importance, even in a secular society, as it is one of the keys to helping everyone to get along with each other.

BIBLE STORIES

There are lots of Bible stories that can be used to illustrate forgiveness. The account of Jesus forgiving the people who nailed him to the cross (Luke 23:34–35) is a particularly vivid one. There is a version of this story in *The Lord's Prayer Unplugged* by Lucy Moore (Barnabas, 2004), which looks at the events from the point of view of a young girl in the crowd.

Other stories include accounts of people whom Jesus healed after forgiving their sins (such as in Matthew 9:1–8 and Mark 2:1–13) and the parable of the official who refused to forgive (Matthew 18:21–35). The latter could be told with the help of audience participation—for example, by using responses to each of the following key words:

* **King**: Your majesty   * **Begging**: Ple-e-e-ase
* **Money**: Chink, chink   * **Official**: Yes, sir!
* **Pay**: Kerching

DISPLAYS FOR THE CHURCH

The craft suggestions below, for decorating wooden crosses, splatter painting and weaving, could all be used to make a larger display for church. For the weaving, just use a larger, sturdier frame; the splatter painting could be done on a prepared board, using much larger-scale shapes; and the cross decorating could be done on a large cross made from boxes (half wine crate size is excellent), fastened together with very strong glue in a cross shape.

CRAFT ACTIVITIES

DECORATING WOODEN CROSSES

> **You will need:** wooden crosses; acrylic paint; small brushes.

Chat about it

Chat about the cross as a symbol for Christianity. In what ways is the cross a powerful symbol of God's forgiveness?

Make it

Small wooden crosses suitable for this activity are obtainable via the Internet or from Christian bookshops that have a merchandise department. Give each child a cross. Invite the children to use the acrylic paint to decorate their cross in whatever way they choose. The children can take their crosses home as a reminder of God's forgiveness.

SPLATTER PAINTING

You will need: some large sheets of paper (perhaps cut from a roll of lining wallpaper); poster paint; brushes for splattering, or plant spray bottles; paper shapes of crosses, keys and chains (if desired); polythene sheeting; aprons; sticky tack.

Chat about it

Chat about how we can feel when we are freed from guilt by being forgiven.

Make it

This is a very liberating way of doing art, and great fun. It can be adapted to other themes but crosses, keys and chain shapes seem suited to forgiveness.

First of all, spread the polythene sheeting over the area where paint might get splattered. Give each child an apron and a large sheet of paper. If you are using pre-cut shapes, invite the children to lay them over the paper in whatever pattern they choose. You may need to weigh the shapes down or use a little sticky tack to keep them in place.

Next, give the children the means of splattering the paint. With large brushes, the children will need to flick them; nail brushes will need to be scraped with a piece of wood or stiff plastic (scraping towards the user, so that the paint sprays away). If you are using spray bottles, experiment first to get the right dilution of paint. The results will depend on how fine a splatter can be obtained. If it is too runny, the paint will run underneath the pre-cut shapes (if you are using them), and it will be impossible to move the artwork for several hours. It is also a good idea to limit the colours available to three or four.

If you are using paper shapes, once one colour has been splattered, move the shapes and splatter with the next colour, and again with the next, always making sure the paint isn't too watery. In this way you will achieve a layered effect. If you don't wish to use shapes to mask areas of the paper, you will still achieve an abstract 'Jackson Pollock' sort of effect.

WEAVING

> **You will need**: frames for weaving (shallow boxes work well; old picture mounts are also good); string; strips of fabric or wool; a hole punch or other method for making holes. **NB**: If you are making a large-scale display, you will need a large frame that has been prepared beforehand with tightly strung piano wire or string.

Chat about it

While engaged in this activity, chat with the children about how our lives are interwoven with each other's. We are interdependent and need to forgive others in the same way that God forgives us for the wrong things that we do.

Make it

Make holes along two opposite sides of the box or weaving frame. You will need to make enough holes to support an odd number of threads fixed across the frame (see diagram).

Invite the children to use the fabric strips or wool to weave in and out of the threads. If you are using fabric strips, you may need to experiment to find the appropriate width; it will depend on how far apart the threads are and how big your frame is. You will also need to show children that each strip is woven in the opposite way to the previous row.

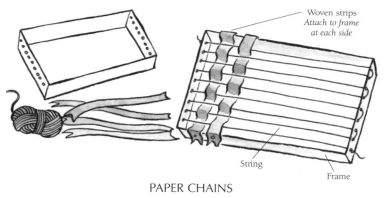

PAPER CHAINS

You will need: gummed paper chain strips.

Chat about it

Chat about the fact that chains are often used as a metaphor for the way we can be ensnared by sin. Making paper chains gives an opportunity to talk about this with the children. Use the chains later for the prayer idea at the end of this chapter.

Make it

Get all the children involved in making up the paper chains and then string them up safely for use at the end of the session.

CROSS-STITCH TAPESTRY

You will need: tapestry canvas (cut into cross shapes or with cross shapes marked); tapestry or darning needles with large eyes; scissors; wool.

Chat about it

Chat about the symbolism of the cross shape, and also the fact that each cross-stitch looks like the way we sign a kiss on a card or letter.

Make it

Mark out crosses on the tapestry canvas, or cut the canvas into cross shapes. (If you do the latter, you will need to bind the edges so that they don't unravel.) Show the children how to make cross-stitches and invite them to decorate their canvas with cross-stitches. The stitches can be made at random in lots of different colours; they don't have to be in neat rows.

PRINTING KEYS

You will need: different key shapes cut from foam and glued to card backing to make printing blocks; acrylic paint; rollers, thin sponges or brushes; paper.

Chat about it

Talk about being forgiven for something we have done wrong: perhaps it is like being given a key to get us out of prison, or like someone using a key to open a pair of handcuffs that we are wearing. Ask the children to imagine how this would feel, and chat about times when they have been forgiven or have forgiven someone else.

Make it

Give each child some paper and paint. Invite them to use a roller, sponge or brush to apply paint to the key-shaped print blocks, to print their own picture. They could try to make a specific shape, such as a person or animal, or they could just make an abstract design.

GAMES

CHOCOLATE POTS

You will need: chocolate money or small wrapped chocolate sweets; playing cards; IOU slips.

Chat about it

Talk to the children about how it feels to owe someone money that has to be paid back. What does it feel like to be in debt to someone else? What would it feel like if you were let off that debt?

Play it

Sit the children in a circle and distribute the chocolate fairly between them (three or four pieces each). Ask each child to place one piece of chocolate in the middle of the circle. Show them the pack of cards and explain that aces are high, red cards are higher than black, and pointy cards are higher than round ones (so diamonds are higher than hearts and spades are higher than clubs). Give each child a card, placing it face down in front of them. Invite the children to turn their card over. The player with the highest card takes all the chocolate in the middle. Once a few rounds have been played, some children will be left with no chocolate, but players are then allowed to write IOUs and place them in the middle instead. Play a few rounds. Then ask if the children who have 'won' the IOUs are prepared to tear the slips up, forgive the debt and redistribute the chocolate. You may be able to prevail upon them to share the chocolate fairly!

IT AIN'T HEAVY

You will need: paper; pens; a bag or suitcase packed with a number of items, some of which might be needed to go on a journey (such as a passport, money or a map). Make sure there are also some heavy, unnecessary items that would only get in the way (such as a pair of boots, a brick or a melon).

Chat about it

Open the suitcase and look at what's inside. Talk to the children about what they might need to take with them on a journey and what might be better left behind. Invite the children to try carrying the bag, first with all the items inside and then with the superfluous ones removed. Talk about how being forgiven by God is a bit like that. God takes away all the unnecessary burdens we carry around: once we are forgiven, we can leave our sins behind and carry on without them.

Play it

Use the items to play Kim's game by shutting the case and seeing how many items the children can remember. Depending on the age of the children, you could use either all the items or just the necessary ones.

PRAYERS

FORGIVE-O-MATIC

You will need: a washing machine front made from a cardboard box with a door that opens; two white T-shirts; felt-tipped pens. You could label the machine a 'Forgive-o-matic' if you wished!

Make sure one of the T-shirts is behind the machine, or held out of sight in a bag taped to the inside.

Talk to the children about forgiveness and how forgiveness is like God washing us clean again and taking our sin away. Show the children one of the white T-shirts and invite them either to mark it with pens (if they are very young) or to write or draw something they want to say sorry to God for. Once the T-shirt has been passed round all the children, open the door of the machine and put the dirty garment into the machine. Say a general prayer saying 'sorry' to God and asking for forgiveness. You might like to leave a little time for children also to say their own private prayer. Then, as a symbol to show them what God's forgiveness can be like, take the clean T-shirt out of the machine.

PAPER CHAIN PRAYERS

You will need: gummed paper chain strips.

If the children have made paper chains earlier, you can use them in the prayers. If they haven't already made paper chains, give out the paper strips and make a chain together. Sit the children in a circle and say a general prayer asking God for forgiveness. Then, as a physical sign of God's forgiveness, break the chains apart. Lay the broken chains in the centre of the circle and finish by saying the Lord's Prayer together.

ACTIVE CONFESSION

Leader: When we come to say sorry to God, we can say it in a very special way.

First of all, we touch the palm of each hand to say sorry for the wrong things we have done this week.

All touch palms with the first two fingers of the other hand.

Leader: Then we touch our eyes to say sorry for the wrong things we have seen.

All touch eyes.

Leader: Then we touch our ears to say sorry for the wrong things we have listened to.

All touch ears.

Reproduced with permission from *Through the Year with Jesus!* published by BRF 2009 (978 1 84101 578 1)
www.barnabasinchurches.org.uk

Leader: Then we touch our mouths to say sorry for the wrong things we have said.

All touch mouth.

Leader: Then we touch our forehead to say sorry for the wrong things we have thought.

All touch forehead.

Leader: Then we touch our hearts to say sorry for the wrong things we have felt.

All put right hand to chest.

Leader: When we say sorry to God, he forgives us for all the times we have turned away from him and wraps us in the warmth of his love.

All wrap arms around the body in a hug.

Leader: Thank you, Lord God, for your love.
All: Amen

Reproduced with permission from *Through the Year with Jesus!* published by BRF 2009 (978 1 84101 578 1)
www.barnabasinchurches.org.uk

Theme 8

TRANSFIGURATION:
THE TRUE GLORY OF JESUS

KEY BIBLE FOCUS: MARK 9:2–8

The celebration of the transfiguration falls on 6 August and is often missed because it occurs in the middle of the summer holidays. If your group has a break over the summer, you might consider exploring this important event with the children in either July or September.

Coming immediately after Peter's declaration that Jesus is the Messiah (Mark 8:29), the transfiguration is a pivotal point in the Gospel narrative. It is a turning point not just for Peter but also for Jesus as he makes up his mind to go to Jerusalem (Luke 9:51) and the rejection that awaits him. The story of the transfiguration is recorded in all three of the Synoptic Gospels (Matthew 17:1–8; Mark 9:2–8; Luke 9:28–36).

Read the story to the children, either from a suitable Bible such as the CEV, or from a children's Bible such as *The Barnabas Children's Bible* (Barnabas, 2007). Alternatively, you could tell the story in your own words. Whichever method you choose, make sure you emphasize the 'awe and wonder' aspect of the story—for example, by lingering on how the disciples who witnessed the event must have felt at the time and also speculating on how Jesus felt. Talk with the children about the fact that this is the moment in Jesus' journey when he makes up his mind to leave Galilee and head for Jerusalem.

The Bible tells us that the transfiguration shows us the true glory of Jesus. John tells us that Jesus' glory was shown at the wedding in Cana (John 2:11). What might it have meant for those with Jesus at the time when he showed his glory? What might it mean for us today?

DISPLAYS FOR THE CHURCH

Talk to the children about how caterpillars change into butterflies. You could mention that sometimes butterflies are used as a metaphor for Jesus' resurrection. Jesus' transfiguration wasn't quite the same because Jesus went back to being the man the disciples knew, but, just for a moment, they glimpsed who he really was. When we look at caterpillars, we can remember what they have potential to be.

You will need: garden netting; card shapes for caterpillars, butterflies and pupae; poster paint or collage materials; glue; stapler; strips of green fabric; crêpe and tissue paper.

Show the children some pictures of all three stages of the butterfly's life cycle and invite them to use the card shapes of butterflies, caterpillars and pupae to make their own creatures. You could use paint or collage for this. When the shapes are dry, suspend the garden netting from somewhere convenient in your venue (you may need something to weigh it down so that it hangs properly). Then thread a selection of fabric strips, crêpe paper and tissue paper in various shades of green in and out of the netting. You should achieve a camouflage effect. The decorated shapes can then be attached to the netting using a stapler, making sure that you catch the strands of netting when attaching the shapes. Carefully, transport the finished work to your church for display.

CRAFT ACTIVITIES

TRANSFORMING MIRRORS

You will need: flexible plastic mirrors cut to A5 size; acrylic paint; brushes; small stickers; glitter glue (optional).

Chat about it

Talk to the children about how people are not always as they appear to be. Sometimes you have to look further or ignore something on the surface to find out what a person is really like. During the event known as the transfiguration, Jesus was transformed so that, for a moment, the disciples saw not only the person of Jesus but also his divinity.

Make it

Invite the children to look into the mirror and mark roughly where their faces appear using the small stickers. They can then use the paints to create something around the face so that, when they look in the mirror, they are transformed. For instance, they might wonder what they would look like wearing a crown, with a halo, or sporting a moustache.

PHOTO-SENSITIVE PAPER

You will need: photo-sensitive paper; objects that can be laid flat to make patterns; a bowl of water; a watch with a second hand.

Chat about it

The story of the transfiguration talks about Jesus' face changing and his clothes shining white (Luke 9:29). Mark's Gospel says that his clothes became 'whiter than any bleach on earth could make them' (Mark 9:3). Talk to the children about what happens when we leave things in the sun. The sun will bleach wood and fabrics, but Jesus' clothes were even whiter than this.

Make it

The success of this activity will depend on how bright the sun is. If the day is dull, or your room is dark and you are unable to put the papers outside, you may need to wait for a sunny day.

Before the session starts, check the instructions for using the paper. It is also a good idea to experiment beforehand to ascertain the correct exposure time for that day. Ask the children to plan a design that could be made by arranging the objects on the paper. Give out the paper and invite the children to create their design as quickly as possible (since as soon as the paper is taken out of the envelope, the exposure will start). Leave the papers out in the sun. After the correct exposure time, rinse the papers in water and leave them to dry.

You will need: shallow sturdy boxes; card; glue; scissors; pastels.

Chat about it

Show the children some pictures of skies so that they can see how different the sky can look at different times. Discuss the way clouds can make a difference to the feel of the sky. Talk about how the sky might have looked from the high mountain top on the day of the transfiguration.

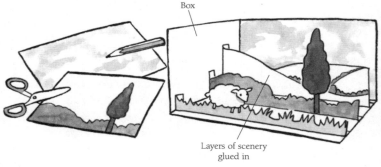

Box

Layers of scenery glued in

Make it

Invite the children to use their box to create a small scene using layers of card. If they wish, they can shade the scenery using the pastels, but coloured card will do just as well. Add layers of scenery going backwards in the box: there might be a figure in the foreground and a couple of layers of background behind it—trees and bushes, with hills behind them. On two separate pieces of paper, ask the children to draw skies using the pastels—one sky on a fine day and the other on a stormy day. These skies can drop down behind all the scenery and will completely change the mood of the scene.

PICTURE PUZZLES

You will need: picture puzzles (probably eight or ten) made by mounting images of well-known people on to stiff card; further sheets of stiff card; scissors.

Chat about it

Chat about the fact that the disciples were used to going up into the mountains with Jesus, where they could be away from the crowds. Jesus would often use these times to be quiet with God and to pray. Luke says that it was while Jesus was praying that his face was completely changed (Luke 9:29). Talk to the children about what it is in people's faces that helps us to recognize them. In what ways may the disciples have found it difficult to recognize Jesus when his face was shining 'like the sun' (Matthew 17:2)?

Play it

Choose some pictures of famous people (make sure they are people or characters that the children are likely to know, such as the Queen, Prime Minister, sporting heroes, pop stars and so on. The Internet is a good source for images, but magazines and newspapers will also have some that you can use. You will need to prepare the pictures in advance by mounting them on stiff card.

For each picture, cut out a rectangle from the middle of another piece of card to make a frame. Then cut the rectangle into jigsaw-like pieces and replace the whole lot on top of the picture.

When you are ready to play the game, invite one child at a time to choose and remove one piece from the jigsaw. Supervise the removal of each piece to ensure that all the other pieces stay in place. As the pieces are removed, the children try to guess who the famous person is. If you want to make a competitive game of this, you could award five points for a correct guess after only one piece of the puzzle is removed. Guesses thereafter would earn one point less for each piece of card removed.

WHOSE FEET?

You will need: a screen, blanket or curtain held just off the floor so that feet and ankles are visible behind it.

Chat about it

Talk about the fact that the disciples knew and worked with Jesus, but they didn't witness his true glory except in very brief, isolated moments. It is like recognizing someone by only seeing a very small part of them.

Play it

This game is great fun. Ask all the children (and adults) to remove their shoes and socks (or just their shoes if the children are reluctant to remove their socks). Depending on the size of your group, pick two or three children at a time to be guessers. Seat the rest of the children behind the blanket, curtain or screen and mix them around. The guessers then have to try to guess who is who, just from seeing the feet. After each round, change the guessers so that everyone has a turn.

WHO AM I?

You will need: cards showing names and descriptions of well-known characters from books, films or TV programmes.

Chat about it

This game is similar to the picture puzzle game above and can be introduced in a similar way.

Play it

Before your session, you will need to prepare a series of cards, each with the name of a well-known character from a book, film or TV programme and a clue as to the character's identity. For example, a card for Spiderman might also say 'Film character beginning with S who wears a disguise'. Invite each child in turn to take a card and read the clue (but not the name of the character). The other children have to guess who the character is. The child then suggests further clues as necessary until the correct identity is guessed.

PRISMS

You will need: prisms and torches (the prisms will need to be of good quality so that they separate the light, and the torches should produce a narrow but bright beam of light).

Chat about it

Show the children how prisms can be used to separate white light into a spectrum of colours. Talk to the children about how all the colours of the rainbow are in light all the time, but we don't see them until we separate them out. Jesus' transfiguration was a bit like a prism for the disciples. Suddenly, instead of the ordinary (white light) person they could see the extraordinary full spectrum of God.

Play it

Allow the children to experiment with the light and prisms for a while. See if the white light can be recombined by using a second prism. You could add mirrors, too, if you wished.

SEEING THINGS IN A NEW LIGHT

> **You will need:** ultraviolet light (it is possible to buy torches that have an ultraviolet light); bank notes.

Chat about it

Show the children an ordinary bank note, then shine an ultraviolet light on to it and see what happens. The markings on the bank note are there all the time, but they only show up under ultraviolet light.

Play it

Allow the children to experiment with the ultraviolet light and the bank notes.

OPTICAL ILLUSIONS

You will need: a selection of pictures showing optical illusions (the Internet is a good place to find images).

Show the children the pictures and ask them what they see. Answers may vary, but often people see only one image to start with. Point out the alternative image so that the children can see that both are there.

Next, read Matthew 25:35–40. Pray with the children that we will be able to see the extraordinary in the ordinary, and that we will be able to see Jesus wherever we go and in everyone we meet.

Theme 9

JESUS' FRIENDS: COME WITH ME!

KEY BIBLE FOCUS: MARK 1:16–20

The stories about Jesus' friends help us to imagine Jesus in the setting in which he lived. By way of introduction, chat with the children about the importance of friendships and what it feels like to have a friend. It is sometimes said that the best way to have a friend is to be a friend, and this thought would make a good introductory discussion. You could also talk about the different people whom Jesus chose, and still chooses, to be his friends.

BIBLE STORIES

Tell the story of Jesus choosing the four fishermen (Luke 5:1–11). The story lends itself well to a visual telling, such as showing a video clip or simply retelling the story in your own words with some pictures or visual aids.

Other related stories include the story of Jesus choosing Philip and Nathanael (John 1:43–51) and Levi (Luke 5:27–32), Jesus' visit to Mary and Martha (Luke 10:38–42), and Peter's vision of the cloth full of animals (Acts 10:1–48), which illustrates God's concern to reach all people, no matter who they are or what their background is.

Talk to the children about how Jesus chose his disciples (some of whom were fishermen) and how their lives were changed by being friends with Jesus.

You will need: a large piece of black card or paper mounted on to a solid board; holographic paper cut into circles; PVA glue; squares of coloured paper from magazines; fishing net (optional).

With the children, decide on a design for a fishy picture (you could either have one large fish or a number of smaller ones). Draw the design in pencil on to the prepared black card or paper backing and decide which colours should go where. Invite the children to stick the holographic paper on to the picture to make the fish. The circular pieces of holographic paper should overlap to form 'scales'. Invite to stick the coloured paper squares on to make the background. Gaps should be left between the squares for a mosaic effect.

You will need to size the circular pieces of holographic paper and the squares of coloured paper according to the scale of your design.

If you have used a number of fish shapes, you might want to finish the mosaic by draping some netting over part of it.

MULTIRACIAL DISPLAY

You will need: ready-cut face shapes; paint and brushes, or collage materials and PVA glue; display board or lining wallpaper.

This activity relates well to the story of Peter's vision of the cloth full of animals (Acts 10:9–16). Allow the children to choose their ready-cut face base and then invite them to create a face using either painting or collage techniques. Make sure you end up with lots of different sorts and colours of faces. The children could make more than one each if required. The faces can be mounted on a display board or used to make a frieze. Copy out a suitable Bible verse, such as Acts 10:34–35, as a title.

CRAFT ACTIVITIES

FISHING FOR PEOPLE MOBILE

You will need: fish shapes; foil; tissue paper; scissors; PVA glue; string; sticks or canes.

Chat about it

This activity allows plenty of time to talk about Jesus choosing his first disciples, and what Jesus meant when he said, 'I will teach you how to bring in people instead of fish' (Matthew 4:19).

Make it

Give the children some of the fish shapes and encourage them to turn them into a fishy collage using foil and tissue paper. Overlapping the materials will give a more interesting effect. Decorate both sides.

Allow the collage fish to dry, then fold them in half horizontally and make four or five cuts across the body of the fish, making sure the cuts don't go to the edge. Fold the slits alternately to the back and front to give the fish a more three-dimensional appearance. Attach the string or thread and hang the fish from the canes.

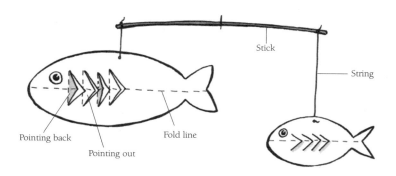

CLAY HANDPRINTS

You will need: clay; instructions for home baking; a surface suitable for rolling; an old rolling pin. (You can use air-drying clay, if preferred.)

Chat about it

This activity and the one below give the children an opportunity to think about how they use their hands. Both activities work well with the story of Mary and Martha.

Make it

Give each child a lump of clay and demonstrate how to roll it out. Make sure it is not too thin (optimum thickness will depend on the type of clay). Show the children how to press their hands into the clay to make a print impression, and then invite them to make their handprints. Ask the children to engrave their names in the clay and (if desired and there is room) add decorations round the print. If you are using clay that needs to be baked, make sure you have home baking instructions to give to the children's parents. Clay usually takes a long time to bake at a low heat, so you will probably not have time to bake it during the session.

HANDPRINT PICTURES

You will need: a large sheet of card; poster paint in trays; brushes or sponges; hand-washing equipment.

Chat about it

Talk about what we use our hands for. Examples might include praying, giving, receiving, playing, waving, making, painting, working, eating and so on. Then decide together on a design that would lend itself to a handprint picture, such as a tree, a flower or a fish.

Make it

Mark out the chosen design on a large sheet of card. Invite the children to make their handprints on the design (preferably in the appropriate place, and using the appropriate colour). Think about the shape of the hands when the children are doing this so that they emphasize the design. For example, fingers could echo the petals of sunflowers or the spreading of leaves on a tree. If you are making a fish, you could have the heel of the hand towards the front and the fingers pointing to the back of the fish (the direction of swim).

Refer back to your discussion about what we use our hands for and invite the children to write one idea in each handprint. Older children may want to write the ideas themselves; younger children may need adult assistance.

SOCK PUPPETS

You will need: a pair of socks for each child; PVA glue; fabric and felt scraps; wool.

Chat about it

Chat about what it feels like to be a brother or a sister. Lead on to talk about the story of Martha and Mary. In what ways were the two sisters similar to our own families? In what ways were they different?

Make it

Show the children how to make a sock puppet. Take the toe of a sock and tuck it inside, folding it back towards the heel to form the nose and mouth. Show the children a finished puppet to help them understand how the puppet works. Invite the children to use the fabric and felt scraps and wool to glue on the

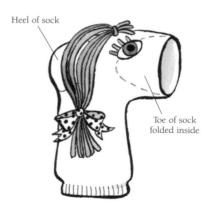

Heel of sock

Toe of sock folded inside

features for their puppets (hair, eyes, nose and mouth). Allow the sock puppets to dry. In pairs, use the puppets to act out the rivalry between Mary and Martha.

BOOKMARKS

You will need: pressed flowers and leaves; PVA glue; ready-cut card bookmark shapes; a laminator; laminating pouches; embroidery thread; a ready-made example.

Chat about it

Chat about Jesus and his friends and the things they did together. Talk about the things the children enjoy doing with their own friends.

Make it

Show the children a ready-made bookmark that you have designed and laminated. Then invite the children to use the pressed flowers and leaves to make their own designs on the bookmark shapes. Glue the flowers in place. Choose a verse from the story you have used or a paraphrase (for example, for the Mary and Martha story, you might choose 'Mary has chosen what is best': Luke 10:42). Invite the children to write the verse or paraphrase on the back of their bookmark.

Place the bookmarks in laminating pouches, making sure there is sufficient space between them to enable them to be separated later, and laminate them. Cut the laminating pouch to separate the bookmarks. Punch a hole in the bottom end of the bookmark. Make a tassel with embroidery thread and attach it to the bookmark.

NB: Laminators show the children's work to good effect and you may be able to borrow one if you do not already have one.

ICHTHUS

Chat about it

Show the children the Christian fish symbol and ask if they have seen it before. Talk about the fact that early Christians were often treated very badly because they were followers of Jesus. Explain how they used the symbol of the fish as a secret sign, so that they could identify other Christians.

Make it

Cut out some pieces of card and write the words in Greek on the front of the card, with a translation on the back.

Slide the cards one over the other to reveal the Greek word *ICHTHUS*. There may be a child in your group who is a dinosaur fan and knows about ichthyosaurs.

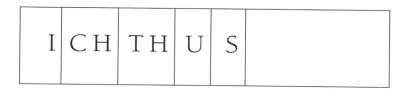

> **You will need**: ingredients for making the recipe of your choice (selected from the recipes below or recipes of your own); bowls and wooden spoons; paper plates; hand-washing equipment; written consent from the parents concerning the activity and information about allergies.

Chat about it

Chat about times when the children eat with their friends. What does it feel like to share a meal with someone special? Think about the times when Jesus ate with his friends, such as the story of Martha and Mary (Luke 10:38–42), or the story of the breakfast on the beach (John 21:1–14).

Make it

Ask the children to wash their hands before they handle any of the cooking ingredients. Choose one of the recipes below. Make the food and enjoy it together.

> **For Krispie rice cakes, you will need**: 100g plain chocolate; 6 tbsp cocoa; 6 tbsp golden syrup; 100g puffed rice cereal; a microwave to melt the chocolate, or a ready supply of hot water; paper cake cases.

Melt the chocolate, milk and golden syrup in a bowl in the microwave, or stir over a pan of hot water. Make sure the children are kept well away from anything hot while you do this. When the chocolate mixture is melted, stir in the puffed rice. Then spoon the mixture into fairy cake cases and leave to set.

For fruit punch, you will need: some large plastic jugs; cranberry juice; apple juice; red grape juice or pomegranate juice; lemonade; a large plastic spoon; plastic cups or beakers.

Mix the fruit juices together in the jugs. Stir in the lemonade. Pour into cups to serve.

For iced fairy cakes, you will need: ready-made fairy cakes (either bought or homemade); icing sugar; water; lemon juice; sugar sprinkles. Quantities will depend on how many cakes you are icing.

Prepare the icing by mixing a little water into the icing sugar, making sure it is not too thin (it shouldn't run off the cakes). Add a little lemon juice to help take the edge off the sweetness. Invite the children to spread the icing over the cakes and decorate with the sugar sprinkles.

For sandwiches, you will need: bread (sliced is easiest); food preparation boards; spread; jam or other fillings such as Marmite, cheese or ham; knives; paper plates.

Encourage the children to butter the bread and then add the fillings. Cut up the sandwiches. Depending on their age and experience, the children may need help with this. When the sandwiches are cut into sensible-sized pieces, put them on plates to serve.

For apple boats, you will need: apples; knives; lemon juice; pastry brush; chopping boards; cocktail sticks; paper triangles (holographic paper looks very exciting).

Wash, quarter and core the apples in advance, brushing the apples with lemon juice to delay browning. Show the children how to slide the paper triangles on to the cocktail sticks and fix them in the apple quarters. The apples will look like boats with sails.

GAMES

BLINDFOLD OBSTACLE COURSE

You will need: plenty of space; comfortable blindfolds such as soft scarves; equipment to make an obstacle course, such as cones, a soft foldaway tunnel, hoops, chairs, and so on.

Chat about it

Talk to the children about the importance of trusting our friends and how our relationship with God also needs to be built on trust. When we are unsure what is ahead, we need to trust God to guide us through the decisions we have to make. Trust in God is a key part of being a friend of Jesus.

Play it

Make an easy obstacle course with, for example, cones to weave in and out of, a tunnel to crawl through, some soft stepping stones or hula hoops to climb through. The children take it in turns to be blindfolded and taken by a trusted friend (or an adult) through the obstacle course. The person leading needs to talk the blindfolded child through the course, taking care to move slowly and carefully. If there is anything that needs to be stepped over, this needs to be supervised to keep the child safe and stable.

HOT-SEATING

You will need: a copy of a story, such as the story of Martha and Mary (Luke 10:38–42); hats for each character (if desired).

Chat about it

Read the story to the children and talk about it briefly. If the children have not had a go at hot-seating before, an adult may need to show them what they need to do.

Play it

Invite one person to sit on the hot-seat and take the role of one of the characters in the story. If it helps for them to wear the appropriate hat, that's fine. The other children then ask the hot-seated child questions about what happened, how they felt, what they wanted and so on. The hot-seated child answers in character. This is a good way to help children to explore the story in some depth.

Alternatively, use the story of Jesus choosing his first friends and hot-seat the disciples in the story (see Bible story references on page 114). Talk about the type of people the first friends of Jesus were. What was their profession? Why did Jesus choose them? Finish by thinking about whether Jesus would have chosen us if we had been there.

PRAYERS

GOD LOVES...

> **You will need**: small pieces of coloured paper; pens; PVA glue; a background picture.

In his dream in Acts 10:1–48, Peter realized that the church was for everyone, no matter where they came from or who they were. Explore with the children the idea that Jesus died for everyone, not just for people of the Jewish or Christian faiths.

Provide small pieces of coloured paper on which the children can write or draw different types of people whom God loves—the people for whom Jesus died. Ask the children to stick these papers on to a picture. You might ask them to fill in the outline of a heart with a heading such as 'God loves us all'. Perhaps they could have sheep-shaped pieces of paper to put into a field, or stick them on to a cross with 'Jesus died for us all' as the title.

Theme 10

JESUS AND ME: LOVE ONE ANOTHER

KEY BIBLE FOCUS: JOHN 15:12–17

Running some sessions that focus on the children themselves can be an excellent way of getting to know the children a little better. Children are usually very happy to talk about themselves, their friends, and what they like and don't like. Make sure you join in, too, so they can get to know you as well. It is an easy step then to encourage children to think about themselves in relation to God.

BIBLE STORIES

A number of Bible passages work well for this theme. You might consider the passage about Jeremiah and the potter (Jeremiah 18:1–6) for older children and Isaiah's passage about God knowing each of us by name (Isaiah 43:1–7) for the younger ones. Psalm 139:1–18 would also be appropriate.

DISPLAYS FOR THE CHURCH

Children like to take their work home, particularly when it is about themselves. However, the silhouettes or activity figures, both of which appear in the craft activities, would make a good church display or frieze.

CRAFT ACTIVITIES

DECORATED MIRRORS

You will need: small mirrors or plastic mirrored A4 sheets cut to size; strips of hardboard; emulsion paint; PVA glue; items to decorate frames, such as fake jewels, beads, painted pasta, and so on.

Chat about it

Talk to the children about the fact that each of us has a unique relationship with God and, as individuals, we are each loved and valued by him. When the children have made their mirrors, they can use them as an aid to a meditation on themselves.

Make it

Framing and decorating mirrors is an excellent activity for this theme. Beforehand, make sure the hardboard pieces are cut to size so that a mirror fits on each one with a margin of roughly 4cm all round. Paint the hardboard with white emulsion to give a good key and then glue the mirrors into place.

Give the children the mounted mirrors and let them get on with decorating them by gluing fake jewels or other decorative pieces to the hardboard margin round the mirror.

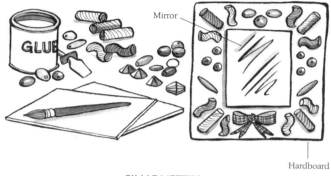

SILHOUETTES

You will need: an anglepoise lamp on a table; easel or other means to hold paper in a near-vertical position; large sheets of paper (black or white); pencil; scissors; large sheets of coloured card; PVA glue; drawing materials.

Chat about it

Talk to the children about the things that matter to them as individuals.

Make it

Position a chair between the lamp and the easel. Put a sheet of paper on the easel and invite each child in turn to sit on the chair, side on to the easel. Shine the light on the side of the child's face and ask an adult helper to draw round the outline of the child's profile. Use a fresh sheet of paper for each child until all the children have an outline of their profile.

Help the children to cut out their profiles and mount them on to card. This works with either white or black paper; either is effective mounted on to coloured card. The children can illustrate themselves further by drawing pictures of things that matter to them round the outlines of their heads. If you are using black paper, try using coloured chalks or soft pastels to do this.

GINGERBREAD PEOPLE

You will need: enough gingerbread dough for the number of children (made in advance or, if time allows, made by the children); baking parchment; baking trays; people-shaped cutters; small rolling pins; pencils; hand-washing facilities.

For the biscuit mix you will need : 300g plain flour; a pinch of salt; 1 tsp baking powder; 1 tsp ground ginger; 100g butter or margarine; 100g soft brown sugar; 2 eggs; 60g golden syrup; mixing bowl; mixing spoon or hand-held mixer; baking parchment or greaseproof paper; flour; mini chocolate or candy sweets, or currants.

Put the flour, salt, baking powder and ginger into a bowl. Rub in the butter or margarine, then stir in the sugar. Beat the eggs with the golden syrup and add to the mixture. Mix well either by hand or with a hand-held mixer.

Make sure the children wash their hands before the activity. Divide the dough into pieces sufficient for all the children. Have a surface ready for rolling (pieces of well-floured baking parchment or greaseproof paper on your normal table covering work well and are disposable later). The dough should be rolled to a thickness of about 5mm. The biscuits can then be cut out with people-shaped cutters. Decorate with mini chocolate or candy sweets or currants.

Place each biscuit on a square of baking parchment, marked with the child's name, then put the biscuits on a baking sheet and bake them on the spot, if you have kitchen facilities. If you have no such facilities, the children could take them home unbaked with instructions on how to finish them at home. The biscuits will need to be baked in an oven pre-heated to Gas Mark 3 or 160°C for about 18 minutes, but keep an eye on them.

NB: As with any food activity, check whether any child has allergies. As the biscuit recipe has egg in it, make sure the children don't eat the raw dough. You will need hand-washing facilities for before and after this activity; if you have no water connection, a plastic washing-up bowl, water warmed in a kettle, some soap and towels will do just as well as a proper bathroom.

SELF SCULPTURES

You will need: air-drying clay; plastic sheeting to cover surfaces; some modelling implements if desired.

Chat about it

Read the story of Jeremiah in the potter's shop (Jeremiah 18:1–6). Chat to the children about how pots are made. Explain how God is sometimes seen as a potter who moulds us into shape in the same way that a potter moulds the clay and shapes it into a pot.

Make it

Older children in particular might enjoy making sculptures of themselves. The children can model themselves using either their mind's eye or their decorated mirrors, if they have made them (see above).

ACTIVITY FIGURES

> **You will need**: thick card cut out in the shape of body parts (see page 189 for templates); a hole punch; split-pin paper fasteners; drawing materials.

Chat about it

Talk about the different kinds of activities the children enjoy, such as running, jumping, hopping, walking, and so on.

Make it

Have the body parts ready prepared. With the children, use a hole punch and paper fasteners to make jointed models out of the figures. The children can decorate their models and then manipulate the figures to do all sorts of actions. As a church display, you could make a frieze with the figures to show the different kinds of activities the children enjoy.

WHAT'S IN A NAME?

> **You will need**: a book of baby names; sturdy paper; brushes; poster paints.

Chat about it

Look up each child's name in the book and find out what it means. If some of the children have an unusual name that isn't in the book, find out if they have an interesting story to tell about their name.

Make it

Give the children some paint and a brush and ask them to paint and decorate their name on one half of a piece of folded card. When they have finished, fold the other half over their painting while the paint is still wet to get a double image (a bit like a butterfly painting). Open out and leave to dry.

GAMES

CATEGORIES

You will need: a list of categories.

Chat about it

Talk about the fact that we are all different, even though we might seem to be the same. In some ways we can be grouped by who we are, but in other ways we are unique. Chat about the things that make us unique and the things that make us like other people.

Play it

Have two points in your venue (A and B) with an adult at each point. The idea is to get the children to classify themselves into two groups, which will be different each time. For example, send the boys to point A and the girls to point B; then send those wearing jeans to point A and those not wearing jeans to point B; then those whose favourite colour is blue to point A, and those whose favourite colour isn't blue to point B. This game can be played for as long as you like and with children of any age, as there are no winners or losers.

NAME GAME

Chat about it

Chat about the things that are part of our personal identify. God has given us many gifts, which make us who we are. Chat about some of the gifts that the children have. These might be physical things that can be seen (such as a smile, or a sibling), or things that are not immediately obvious (such as our kindness, or the fact that we are good at sport).

Play it

Stand the children in a circle and throw the beanbag from one to another, while saying something about the child who will catch the beanbag, such as 'Jenny has three brothers', or 'Matthew likes dinosaurs'.

PRAYERS

THREE FACTS ABOUT MYSELF

You will need: paper and pencils; candle and matches (optional).

Ask each child to write three facts about themselves which only they will know, but which they are happy to share with others. Give adult help with younger children. When they have finished, put all the papers in a centre pot, draw them out one at a time and read them out loud. See if everyone can guess which information belongs to which child. The papers can be used for prayer by giving thanks to God for who we are. Sit the children in a circle and, if desired, light a candle and invite each child to place their piece of paper near the candle before saying the final prayer.

MEDITATION

You will need: the decorated mirrors the children have made, or some hand-held mirrors.

Encourage the children to look at themselves in the mirror. Help them to understand that they are all unique and that they are all loved by God and part of God's family. Select some verses from Psalm 139 to read quietly as the children meditate on themselves.

NOISY PRAYERS

Try a noisy prayer where the children thank God for their bodies, each line of the prayer having an accompanying action—for example, 'Thank you, Lord, for hands that clap... feet that stamp... fingers that click...' and so on.

THANKSGIVING CONTRIBUTIONS

Invite the children to contribute their own line to a prayer of thanksgiving, thanking God for the things that they are especially good at or enjoy doing. Perhaps they could light a tealight candle as they say their part of the prayer.

Theme 11

GOD WITH US: I WILL BE WITH YOU ALWAYS

KEY BIBLE FOCUS: MATTHEW 28:18–20

When we share the gospel with children, we need to help them to recognize the relevance of the stories in today's world. There is much value in giving children time to consider God in their world today and the ways we can encounter (and recognize) him in the places where we live and the people we meet.

BIBLE STORIES

The key verse of Jesus' promise to be with us always can be unpacked in many ways and is an ideal opportunity to explore the ways in which God is with us today. Matthew tells us that Jesus will be called 'Immanuel', which means 'God is with us' (Matthew 1:23), and the Gospels show us that this was true not just for the duration of Jesus' earthly lifetime, but for all people in all times and throughout eternity. To explore the eternal dimension of Jesus' presence with us today, the Pentecost story is a good place to start (see below). Other passages exploring the theme of God's presence with us are those that speak of his love and care for creation and for us as the stewards of his creation (Psalm 8:6).

You will need: red and orange crêpe paper cut into streamers; a CD of joyful music; CD player.

Practise making a collective sound of wind by breathing out with mouths open, quietly first, then loudly. Then set the scene by telling the children the story of the ascension (Acts 1:4–11). Explain that ten days before the events of Pentecost took place, the disciples had seen Jesus taken up into heaven and had been told to wait in Jerusalem for the coming of the Holy Spirit. They had no idea what that meant, but Jesus had told them to wait expectantly, so that is what they did. Explain that they were waiting in a house in Jerusalem, not knowing what to expect.

Next, explain that the story of Pentecost tells us about the day when God breathed his life and power into Jesus' friends. Tell the story of Pentecost using a contemporary version of the Bible, or the version below.

Ask the children to sit waiting as the disciples did that morning—waiting for the gift of God's Holy Spirit.

Suddenly there was a sound like the wind, coming from the sky and getting closer. It was the sound of God breathing his Holy Spirit into Jesus' loyal friends.

All start quietly breathing out with mouths open.

The sound got louder and louder until the whole house they were in seemed surrounded by the living, moving presence of Almighty God.

Breathe more loudly.

Suddenly, it seemed that tongues of flame flickered out from the breath of God and found each person, resting on each one very gently.

Children wave streamers made from red and orange crêpe paper, finally bringing them to rest on the floor.

Jesus' friends were all filled with God's Holy Spirit. They started praising God and shouting out their love for him. They didn't care what anyone else thought of them. All they wanted to do was to thank him and tell him how much they loved him. They lifted their hands and all started talking at once.

Play some music, or get the children to sing a song with gusto, dancing and waving the streamers as they do so.

Quite a crowd had gathered outside the house, wondering what was going on so early in the morning. Still full of God's Spirit, Jesus' friends rushed out into the streets to share the good news. From that day forward, Jesus has been constantly present in the world through the presence of his Holy Spirit.

Finish the story by emphasizing that the Holy Spirit is God's presence in the world today, making it possible for Jesus to be with us always (Matthew 28:20). His presence makes us sure that we will be given all the good things God has stored up for us and helps us to give God honour and praise (Ephesians 1:13–14).

DISPLAYS FOR THE CHURCH

> **You will need:** a large piece of paper or fabric with the world (as a globe) roughly sketched on to it; heart-shaped stamps (or dense foam pieces, wine corks and PVA glue); shades of blue and green poster paint; paintbrushes.

You can make the heart-shaped stamps yourself by gluing small heart-shaped dense foam pieces on to wine corks. Show the children the rough picture of the world and talk about it—how big it is, where we live on it, and where other people live. Talk about whether God is in any one place more than another, or which part of the world God loves best. Invite the children to brush paint on to their heart-shaped stamps and then apply blue and green colour (in the appropriate areas) to the globe to make a picture of our planet as though seen from outer space.

LOCAL ENVIRONMENT DISPLAY

> **You will need:** garden netting; pre-cut card shapes of flora and fauna found in the churchyard or local environment (such as worms, beetles, butterflies, mice, bats and so on); shapes of gravestones (to add lichen to them), leaves and flowers; poster paint; brushes; stapler; green fabric and crêpe paper; pictures so that children can see what the wildlife looks like (if necessary).

Talk to the children about the glory of creation and the wonderful diversity of God's world. If you wished, you could take the children (properly supervised and having obtained the necessary permission from parents and carers) on a short walk into the local environment. If you have a churchyard, this might be far enough, or perhaps you have a local park or other area where plants and wildlife can be seen. Discuss with the children how many different animals and plants there might be and how they all depend on each other. Talk about how they are all part of God's creation and show his care for the world.

Show the children the pre-cut shapes and invite them to paint or decorate them in whatever way seems appropriate. Use the garden netting to set up a display area. Thread strips of green fabric and crêpe paper through the netting to create an interesting background, then attach the painted shapes by stapling them to the netting.

GOD'S WORLD MOBILE

You will need: large card circles, each with a hole punched at one side; a collection of pictures and collage items; PVA glue; string; a frame made from sticks or garden canes.

Talk about our responsibility to care for God's creation. Show the children the collage items and give each child a large card circle. Invite them to use one side to depict the wonder and diversity of God's creation and the other to show the ways in which we can take care of it. Give the children time to complete their collages. They may need to wait for one side to dry before starting the other. When the circles are ready, they can be suspended with string from the hanging frame.

PAINTED HEART BISCUITS

You will need: biscuit dough (see recipe on page 130, but replace ground ginger with the grated rind of one lemon); red food colouring; round and heart-shaped pastry cutters; rolling pins; clean floured surface; baking sheets; baking parchment; extra egg yolk; small cup; very clean small paintbrush.

Chat about it

Talk about God's care for every part of his creation and how he has given us the responsibility to look after it.

Make it

Unless the children are going to be making the biscuit dough during the session, have enough ready made to give every child a medium-sized piece of dough. Invite the children to roll out the dough to a thickness of 3–5mm and then cut out biscuits using the circular cutters. Ask the children to transfer their biscuits to the sheets of baking parchment, naming the sheets so that the children can identify their own biscuits. Then show the children how they can mark each biscuit with the heart-shaped cutter, being careful not to cut through the whole biscuit. Mix some red food colouring into the egg yolk in a small cup and invite the children to paint the coloured yolk on to each heart shape using a very clean small paintbrush.

Bake for 10–12 minutes or until the biscuits begin to colour round the edges. Cool slightly on the baking sheets before transferring to a cooling rack. The biscuits will have red or pink glazed hearts on them.

MATCHBOX INSECTS

You will need: clean pebbles (small enough to fit into matchboxes); poster paint; brushes; PVA glue; paper, beads, wool and so on to decorate.

Chat about it

Talk about how God's care for us and all living things can be seen all around us, even in creatures we might think of as 'creepy crawlies'. In this activity, the children will be taking some care in their creations, too.

Make it

Ask the children to choose a small pebble and then to decorate it carefully, using the materials to make it look like a small insect, such as a ladybird.

DECORATED MATCHBOXES

You will need: small matchboxes; poster paint; brushes; glitter glue; wool (to wrap around the boxes if desired).

Chat about it

Talk about how God's care for his world shows us that he also cares for us. In fact, Jesus tells us that God cares for us even more than he cares for any other part of his creation (Matthew 6:25–26). How great is God's care for us!

Make it

Invite the children to decorate their matchboxes (making sure they don't glue them shut with glitter glue) to make a good home for their pebble insects.

LEAF COLLAGE

You will need: pressed leaves; paper; PVA glue.

Chat about it

Look with the children at all the different leaves. Examine the different shapes, sizes and colours. Look at how they are veined. With older children you might talk about how leaves work to make food for the plant. Spend some time wondering at it.

Make it

When you have finished examining the leaves, invite the children to use the pressed leaves to make their own pictures. They could choose to make an abstract pattern or depict something from nature. If you have access to a laminator, the pictures could be laminated to preserve them.

If you are using small leaves (and perhaps flowers), you could use the same technique (including lamination) to make bookmarks. On the reverse side, write a Bible verse, such as Matthew 28:18–20.

RECOGNITION

You will need: electronic images (JPEGs) of well-known people; access to a computer; image-altering software.

Chat about it

Read 1 Corinthians 13:12. Talk about how we recognize people we know and can pick them out immediately, even in a crowded room. Explain that God recognizes us because he knows us and, even though we can't see God, we can still know him. One day we will see him face to face.

Play it

Beforehand, select some pictures of people who are very well known, such as the Queen, and film, TV or sporting personalities. Use the software to tamper with the pictures by adding filters that obscure the image. Show the pictures to the children and see if they can guess who the people are. If you have another copy of the image without the filter, you can prove who the people are.

CONSEQUENCES

You will need: paper; pens or pencils.

Chat about it

Think about how God works in the most unlikely ways and places.

Play it

Sit the children in a circle. Ask each person to write someone's name at the top of their piece of paper and then fold over the paper so that the writing is not visible. The papers are then passed on to the next person in the circle, who writes the name of someone whom the first person will meet. The papers are folded again and passed on. The next person decides on a venue for the meeting. The next decides what the first person said to the second person; and the next what the second person replied. The 'coup de grâce' is 'And the consequence was…'. When all the stages have been completed, the consequences can be read as a sequence.

Alternatively, the children can draw a person, starting with the head, then the torso, then the legs and, finally, the feet. This version could be used to illustrate the fact that the family of God (the body of Christ) is made from many parts, but all contribute to the whole (1 Corinthians 12:19–20).

PRAYERS

HAZELNUTS

> **You will need:** hazelnuts in their shells (if these are not available, use something similar, such as conkers, acorns or walnuts); magnifying glasses.

Explain that Julian of Norwich was a devout Christian who lived 600 years ago. She is particularly famous for the way she interpreted dreams and images that God had put into her mind. In one of these, she was shown a small thing the size of a hazelnut in the palm of her hand. In her reflection on this image, she saw that it represented the whole of creation. Julian was told three things about it: God made it, God loves it, and God keeps or cares for it.

Encourage the children to think about the hazelnut sitting in the palm of their hand. Talk about how a tree makes hazelnuts, and why. Look at the nuts under a magnifying glass to see the detail more clearly. When you have spent enough time on this, tell the children about Julian's own reflection and how, for her, the hazelnut represented all creation. Talk about the size and scale of creation, and what size it must seem to God. How big or significant are we within it?

Conclude the meditation with prayers thanking God for his constant watch over us and his care of all that he has made. Give the children the opportunity to spend some time silently remembering that we are a very small but much-loved part of creation and marvelling that this should be so.

You will need: a copy of 'Jesus' blood never failed me yet' by Gavin Bryars (Philips, 1993); a CD player.

Play a short section of the recording to the children and then tell them about how the composer used this simple song of faith, sung by a homeless man, to make an extraordinary piece of music. When they have understood the circumstances surrounding the composition of the piece, listen to a bit more. You could then discuss the piece with the children. What do they think of it? Would they expect someone in this man's situation to be singing such a heartfelt song, and if not, why not? How can someone who has lost everything be so certain of his faith in God? Would they expect to find something of God in someone who was homeless on the streets of a big city?

Finish by turning your thoughts into a prayer about God's presence with those who have nothing. Thank God for the resilience (and even joy) that faith in him gives to people who face terrible situations and circumstances.

SUMMER ACTIVITY
PROGRAMME OR
STAND-ALONE ACTIVITY DAYS

THE 'I AM' SAYINGS OF JESUS: EXPECT THE UNEXPECTED!

The 'I am' sayings of Jesus recorded in John's Gospel make a good focus for a series of activity days for children. The material in this section was first developed as a Lent course for children aged 7–12. The central craft idea for each workshop is the making of one panel each day to form a large hanging for display by the end of the programme (see illustration below). You might want to adapt this idea to make an altar frontal or similar hanging for your church. The completed hanging would make a good visual focus for worship at the end of the programme.

DAY ONE: LIGHTEN UP!

'I am the light for the world!'

KEY BIBLE FOCUS: JOHN 8:12

'I AM' DISPLAY FOR THE CHURCH

> **You will need:** prepared fabric hanging (see page 150); materials required to make the first design (see below); either fabric paints or fabric scraps in different colours; PVA glue.

Divide the hanging into five sections. On the top left-hand section, prepare a design to represent light. This could be either a lit candle with light spreading out (sunbeam-like) to the edges of the design area, or a circle of white in the centre with concentric circles expanding out in gradually darkening shades of yellow, or perhaps rainbow shades. The design could be executed using fabric paint (glittery or pearlized paint would be effective), or you might prefer to use fabric pieces and glue.

DISCUSSION

Read the focus Bible text and discuss with the children why Jesus described himself in this way. What kind of light can we think of? What sort of light did Jesus mean? What would happen if there were no light? Light is not only essential for us to be able to see clearly and to keep warm; we also need it to be able to survive. Plants make their food by photosynthesis so if they were unable to do this, plant life would fail. Herbivores would then die and, consequently, so would carnivores and omnivores.

Talk about how illumination can be not only physical but also spiritual. Is the light that Jesus talked about a physical light or a spiritual one?

CRAFT ACTIVITIES

LIGHTING WITH COLOUR

You will need: illustrations of illuminated manuscripts; paper; fine paintbrushes; artists ink.

Show the children the illustrations and talk about why they are called illuminated manuscripts—exploring the way that the text is decorated, how the technique is used to decorate an initial letter or border, what colours are used and so on. Talk about how important these manuscripts were to the people who made them and read them. Chat about how illuminated manuscripts can shed a spiritual light on the Bible texts.

Invite the children to have a go at making their own illuminated manuscript using brush and ink. Use John 8:12 as the verse to illuminate and see how much detail and how much care can be lavished on these words.

COLOURING THE WORLD WITH LIGHT

You will need: black card or thick paper cut to the world stencil template (see page 190 for a diagram), enough for all the children; coloured cellophane; PVA glue.

Cut the simplified world design stencil from the black card. You could also use the activity to make a display, in which case you will need just one enlarged stencil cut from much tougher card or mounting board.

Invite the children to use the cellophane to fill the spaces, gluing it on the reverse side of the card. When all the parts of the world are coloured with cellophane, allow the glue to dry. The finished design can be placed in the window for the sunlight to shine through.

BEESWAX CANDLES

You will need: sheets of beeswax; candle wick; pizza cutter; metal ruler.

Beeswax sheets and candle wick can be obtained from craft shops or the Internet and can easily be cut using a metal edge and a pizza cutter. Cut sheets of beeswax to whatever size you require, lay the wick along one edge and press it into the wax. Roll the beeswax as carefully and as tightly as you can around the wick to make a candle.

If you have coloured beeswax, experiment with cutting two contrasting sheets into right-angled triangles. Have one triangle a bit smaller than the other and roll them up together with the smaller sheet underneath. You should end up with a two-coloured stripy candle.

CANDLE PAINTING

You will need: plain white or cream ready-made candles; candle paint (obtainable from craft shops or the Internet).

Simply give each child a candle and invite them to decorate it as they see fit.

CERAMIC CANDLE HOLDERS

You will need: ceramic candle holders; ceramic paints; brushes; sponges; a supplier for this craft activity.

There are a number of outlets that allow people to paint their own ceramics. Often someone will either come to your venue or lend you the equipment to take away. This activity does have a cost attached, not just for the materials but also for the glazing and firing, which need to be done by the specialist supplier. However, it does make a very satisfying activity and the reward for the children of seeing their work glazed and fired (after a few days) is very special.

Invite the children to decorate their candle holders. Your specialist supplier will give advice about how best to do this and what to avoid.

FOOD WEB

You will need: a card showing a picture of the sun; further cards showing various plants and animals; lots of string or wool.

This game illustrates the importance of light in all our lives. Depending on the age of the children, you may need to check what they know about how plants get food and you may need to talk a little about photosynthesis. If this is too technical, talk about what happens to plants that are kept in a dark cupboard away from the sun.

You will need a good number of children to make this game work (probably a minimum of ten). Give each child a card. Place the child holding the sun in the middle of the group, with plants around the sun, animals that eat plants further out, and animals that eat other animals round the edge.

Next, the children need to be linked using the string. The sun will hold a number of strings, each of which 'feed' the plants. Plants hold the other end of the string linking them with the sun, and more strings linking to the animals. Some animals may be omnivores, eating both plants and animals, and the strings should reflect this.

When everything is ready, talk about what will happen if one part of the food web fails. This can be illustrated by the relevant organism dropping the strings. Which plants or animals are affected? When you have tried a few combinations, talk about what happens if the light fails. Get the child holding the sun to drop the strings and ask 'Who is affected?'

EXPERIMENTING WITH LIGHT

You will need: overhead projector(s) and screen(s); coloured acetate; objects to make shadow pictures, such as wooden or card shapes, leaf skeletons, feathers, keys and so on.

First of all, make sure the children understand that they must not look into the light source. Encourage them to experiment with making shadows on the screens. They could experiment with coloured filters as well as using objects to make shadow pictures. Take photographs of any images they are satisfied with on the screen.

PRAYERS

PRISM PRAYERS

You will need: prisms or light catchers; a source of light.

Use prisms or crystal light catchers as a focus for prayer. Using the story of Noah's ark could lead nicely into showing how the coloured light of the rainbow is used as a symbol of God's promise. Pray that God's light will help us to see his glory all around us.

TORCHLIGHT PRAYERS

You will need: a strong electric torch; symbols or images to encourage prayer.

If you can darken the room or are holding your prayers at dusk or nightfall, use a strong electric torch to illuminate symbols or images to encourage prayer. Sit the children in a circle with the symbols or images spread out in the centre. Pass the torch around the circle and allow each child in turn to illuminate an object. Match the words of the prayer to the symbol (for example, a star cut from metallic card could be illuminated while thanks are given for the gift of Jesus, or a cross cut from sandpaper while a prayer is said for forgiveness, and so on).

DAY TWO: COME ON IN!

'I am the gate. All who come in through me will be saved. Through me they will come and go and find pasture... I am the good shepherd, and the good shepherd gives up his life for his sheep.'
KEY BIBLE FOCUS: JOHN 10:9 AND 11

'I AM' DISPLAY FOR THE CHURCH

You will need: prepared fabric hanging (see page 150); materials required to make the second design (see below); either fabric paints or fabric scraps in different colours; PVA glue.

On the top right-hand section of the hanging, sketch an open gate, together with sheep. You could use fleecy fabric for the sheep, with black felt for their faces and feet, or faces and feet could be painted on first and the fleece glued on afterwards. The gate could be painted on or made with fabric strips. You could choose to have a fence either side of the gate or perhaps a sponge-painted hedge.

Invite the children to complete the second panel of the hanging.

DISCUSSION

Read John 10:9 ('I am the gate') and talk to the children about gates. What sort of gateways do they know about? What sorts of places have gates and why do they have them? Are gates meant for keeping something in or shutting something out? What do they think Jesus meant by describing himself as a gate?

Next, read John 10:11 ('I am the good shepherd') and explore with the children what a good shepherd might do. Why did Jesus choose to compare himself with a shepherd? If you have a local farm, someone might be prepared to come to talk to the children about what shepherding means now. How would it have been different in Jesus' time and why might a shepherd have been prepared to give up his life for his sheep?

CRAFT ACTIVITIES

SHEEP FRIEZE

You will need: paper for a frieze; sheep-shaped print blocks (see page 191 for a template); poster paint; sponges; brushes.

Sponge some green hills with a sky behind them on to the frieze. When it is dry, invite the children to use white paint and print blocks to print sheep shapes on the landscape. The faces, legs and tails of the sheep can be added later with a brush. Perhaps the children might like to paint their names on the sheep.

GATED SCENERY

You will need: paper; (craft) lolly sticks; pastels; glue (a hot glue gun would be ideal).

Invite the children to use the pastels to draw a landscape— somewhere pleasant where they would like to be. Then ask them to construct a gate (and, if they wish, a fence) using the lolly sticks. If you are using a hot glue gun, they will need help in putting it together. When the picture is finished, the gate can be glued on top of the landscape. Make sure there is no loose pastel on the paper, otherwise the glue may not stick properly.

WELCOME DOOR CARDS

> **You will need:** card; colouring pencils; pens; pictures of doors.

Have the card in front of you in a landscape orientation. Fold one quarter in towards the centre on one side and then on the other, so that the card opens like a set of double doors. Have some pictures of doors to show the children and remind them how different doors can look. Invite the children to use the colouring pencils to make the front of the card look like any sort of doors they wish. Inside the card, they could draw whatever they wanted—perhaps lots of friendly faces—and write a message of welcome. The cards could be given to someone new to the group or community. If you wished, you could make a larger version as a group project to have on display by the entrance to your room.

GAMES

KNOCK, KNOCK!

Seat the children in a group on the floor. From the group choose a doorkeeper who stands at the front with his or her back to everyone else. Then silently choose one of the seated children to say, 'Knock, knock.' The doorkeeper needs to guess who said the words. If the guess is correct, the child who said the words becomes the new doorkeeper, otherwise another child is chosen to say 'Knock, knock.' The children can speak in a way that is different from their normal speaking voice in an effort to put the doorkeeper off the scent.

PRAYERS

DOOR PRAYERS

Use the door to your room as a catalyst for prayer. Perhaps you could stand round the door or entrance, or turn to face it. Pray for those who come in and those who go out.

ASK, SEARCH, KNOCK

Use Matthew 7:7–8 as an inspiration for prayer. Read the verses and invite the children to ask for something from God. They could pray silently or aloud, or may write or draw their prayer to be offered.

DAY THREE: LAY THE TABLE!

'I am the bread that gives life! No one who comes to me will ever be hungry. No one who has faith in me will ever be thirsty... I am the true vine, and my Father is the gardener.'

KEY BIBLE FOCUS: JOHN 6:35 AND 15:1

'I AM' DISPLAY FOR THE CHURCH

> **You will need:** prepared fabric hanging (see page 150); materials required to make the third design (see below); either fabric paints or fabric scraps in different colours; PVA glue.

Sketch a paten and chalice design, complete with bread and wine, on to the bottom left-hand section of the hanging and use the fabric or paints to complete the design. It would be effective to use glittery or pearlized paint for the cup and plate. If it is appropriate, design the paten and chalice to match the vessels you use in your church.

WHEAT AND VINE HANGINGS

> **You will need:** fabric; fabric paint; an old rolling pin; string; wood glue; vine leaves; wine-bottle corks.

If you have curtains around the altar or you have somewhere else to position the display, making these additional hangings is great fun. You could also adapt this idea for the main 'I am' display.

For the wheat hanging, make a print block by gluing string around the rolling pin. Apply gold, yellow or brown fabric paint to the print block and use it to make stalks of wheat. The ears of wheat can be made using fingerprints made in formation and a fine paintbrush to draw the 'hairs' from each grain.

For the vine hanging, use vine leaves (vacuum-packed vine leaves work well and can be obtained from delicatessens). Apply paint to the veined side and use them to make prints. Clusters of grapes can be made effectively by printing in purple paint using corks (appropriately) from wine bottles.

DISCUSSION

Read John 6:35 and talk to the children about what Jesus might have meant when he referred to himself as the bread of life. Why did he choose bread? Introduce the idea that bread was then (and is today) a staple food (you may need to talk a little about what this means). What would happen if a staple food wasn't there? Talk about the importance and the symbolism of people eating a meal together.

Next, read John 15:1 and talk to the children about vines. What grows on them? Why do people grow vines? Bring out the meaning of the plant metaphor: as 'leaves' and 'grapes', we can only flourish and grow if our connection with the vine is good. Talk also about why people drank wine in Jesus' time on earth. (Water was often contaminated but, because of the process required to make wine, it was often safer to drink than water.)

CRAFT ACTIVITIES

MAKING BREAD

> **You will need**: 400g strong plain flour; two level tsp sugar; two level tsp dried yeast (the easy baking variety); 230ml warm water; 1.5 level tsp salt; two tbsp olive oil; two mixing bowls; mixing spoon; sieve; clean tea towel; greaseproof paper; baking tray; cooling rack; oven.

For this activity, you will need hand-washing facilities. If you have no such facilities, a washing-up bowl with warm soapy water and a towel will do just as well. Ensure that the children have clean hands before they begin. Invite them to make the bread together. With kneading and rising time, this will take a while, so you could have a quantity of bread dough ready for the children to shape into rolls or plaits. This could then be shared later in the workshop, or perhaps the next day.

Sift the flour, sugar, yeast and salt into a bowl (if you are using yeast that needs to be reconstituted in water first, follow the instructions on the packet). Add the oil and water and knead well. Cover with a clean tea towel and leave in a warm place for approximately one hour until double in size. Turn out on to a floured surface and knead again evenly until smooth. Divide the dough and shape as required. Place finished products on a greased and floured baking tray. Cover with the tea towel and leave until doubled in size. Bake in the centre of an oven at 375°F, Gas 5 or 190°C for 45–50 minutes for a loaf and 15–20 minutes for rolls, until the top is golden brown and the base sounds hollow when tapped. Cool on a wire rack.

STAPLE FOOD RANGOLI COLLAGE

> **You will need**: sheets of sturdy paper or card; dried staple foods such as different varieties of rice; grains such as wheat and barley; flour; PVA glue; string; spoons.

Talk to the children about staple foods and how they differ in different parts of the world. (In a different part of the world, Jesus might have compared himself to rice instead of bread.) Talk about what bread is made from and how flour is made. Show the children the selection of staple foods and invite them to use them to make pictures. The children could outline their designs by gluing the string to form shapes on their paper; they could then fill in the design using glue and scattering it with the rice or grains (similar to the way glitter is used). If you want a more ephemeral craft activity, use the rice and grains to make a rangoli-type pattern (without glue) on a level place outside (if it is not too windy) such as a doorstep or path.

FAMILY TREES

> **You will need**: large pieces of paper; felt-tipped pens or colouring pencils; a family tree (one of the royal family should be easy to find).

NB: Depending on the children attending your group, some sensitivity may be required when using this activity. If the home life of the children is very disrupted, consider making a spiritual family tree instead.

Show the children a family tree diagram and explain how to read it. Talk about their families and how they might draw a similar diagram. Give each child a large piece of paper and drawing materials and invite them to construct their own family tree. If children preferred, they could draw pictures of their family members instead of writing their names.

If you think it more appropriate to make this activity about a spiritual family tree, ask the children to think of people from whom they have learned about the Christian faith, and ask who might have taught those teachers. They could also think about people whom they have taught or influenced. Set out their spiritual family tree in the same way as a normal family tree.

If you want a more tangible result for this activity, use a twiggy branch 'planted' in a large flower pot. Invite the children to draw pictures of people who have led them on their own spiritual journey and hang the pictures from the branches.

GAMES

SHOPPING LIST GAME

Seat the children in a circle and choose one to begin the game by saying 'When I go to the shops, I need to buy...'. The child adds his or her choice of food to be purchased at the shop. The second child repeats the opening sentence plus the first child's choice, and then adds another item. As each child joins in, the list gets longer. See how many items you can add before someone forgets one of them. You can complicate the game with older children by adding some form of description with each item, such as 'Six rashers of bacon without any rind' or 'A bunch of carrots with the leaves still on them'.

SHARING BREAD

> **You will need:** bread that the children have made, or a bought loaf; a tablecloth; plates; a candle; candle lighter or matches; fire precaution materials.

If you have made bread during the session, you might like to use the opportunity to share it. Alternatively, you could use a shop-bought loaf, making sure it is a 'rustic' variety. Prepare a table with a cloth and plates and light a candle. Say a prayer to thank God for the bread, then break it rather than cutting it. Share it with everyone present and conclude with another prayer, perhaps in relation to spiritual food.

DAY FOUR: WELCOME HOME!

'I am the one who raises the dead to life! Everyone who has faith in me will live, even if they die... I am the way, the truth, and the life!'
KEY BIBLE FOCUS: JOHN 11:25 AND 14:6

'I AM' DISPLAY FOR THE CHURCH

You will need: prepared fabric hanging (see page 150); materials required to make the fourth design (see below); either fabric paints or fabric scraps in different colours; PVA glue.

Sketch a compass design on to the bottom right-hand section of the hanging and use the fabric or paints to complete the design. Point out to the children that joining up the points of the compass (north to south and east to west) makes a cross.

DISCUSSION

Read John 14:6 and talk to the children about the three things Jesus mentions. Talk about what 'the way' might be. How do we find the right way to go or the right way to live? How do we know that something is true? Is life a destination or a journey? How do we know how to live our lives? Next, read John 11:25 and talk about the different people in the Bible who experienced resurrection, such as Lazarus, Jairus' daughter and, of course, Jesus himself. Talk about new life and think about the way that physical new life in spring is like spiritual new life. How do we get 'new' life?

CRAFT ACTIVITIES

LOCAL MAP

You will need: a prepared map of your local area mounted on large board; small pieces of paper.

Talk about the map and identify landmarks on it that everyone will know, such as your church, local schools, shops, the local pub, and so on. Invite the children to use the small pieces of paper to draw common landmarks and then places like houses or dwellings. These can then be stuck on to the map in the appropriate places. When the map is finished, talk about how to get from one place on the map to another.

SUNRISE PICTURE

You will need: very stiff card (mounting board) cut into rectangles measuring approximately 10cm x 15cm; knitting yarns in different colours and textures; double-sided sticky tape; a sample piece.

Sunrise often symbolizes new life. It was at sunrise on the first Easter Day that Jesus was found to have left the tomb. Show the children a prepared example of a sunrise picture and invite them to make their own. Stick double-sided tape to the front and back parallel sides of the mounting board. Then invite the children to wrap the knitting yarns round and round the board to form a picture. For example, they could use a mixture of sandy coloured yarn on the lower third of the board, and then a narrow band of glittery thread, followed by sky shades for the upper two-thirds, to create a desert landscape and sky.

TOPIARY

> **You will need:** flower pots and saucers; garden wire; plug plants (suitable for trailing or climbing); compost.

Topiary is usually made by cutting large hedging plants into shapes, but it can also be achieved by growing climbers over a shaped frame. Let each child fill a flower pot with compost and give them lengths of wire. The degree of supervision required will depend on the ages, maturity and dexterity of the children. Invite the children to shape the wire into whatever shape they wish (perhaps a cross, an egg or a lamb). Sink the ends of the wire into the compost. Let the children plant the plug plants into the pots. As the plants grow, the children can train them round the wires to grow their own topiary shape.

BULBS

> **You will need:** flower pots and saucers; bulbs; compost.

If the time of year isn't suitable for topiary, it might be a good time for planting bulbs instead. Bulbs often seem to be dead but have the wherewithal for new life within them. Allow each child to plant a bulb. With care and water, a new plant will spring up in due course. **NB:** check what precautions need to be taken in handling bulbs (some need to be handled with gloves).

FOLLOWING FOOTPRINTS

You will need: a length of paper (strong lining paper is good); ready-mixed poster paint in different colours; brushes; foot-washing equipment; polythene.

Footprint painting is a great outside painting activity, but can also be done inside if you have enough space and can protect the area around the paper. Lay out the polythene (if needed) and the paper and make sure your foot-washing equipment is to hand. (A washing-up bowl with warm water, soap and towels will be fine.) Invite the children to take off their shoes and socks and paint their feet (be prepared for laughter here). The children can then make their own patterns and paths by walking around on the paper, stopping to repaint their feet when necessary. Including some adult-sized feet and lots of different colours will vary the effect.

GAMES

WHERE NEXT?

You will need: a copy of the Highway Code; paper; marker pens.

Show the children different road signs from a copy of the Highway Code and see if they can work out what the signs might mean. Put the children into pairs and suggest that they take turns to think of something for which a road sign might be needed and draw what it might look like. The other child in the pair then guesses what the sign might be saying. You might need to have some ideas for road signs ready to inspire the children, such as 'Go slower', 'Don't look at the view', or 'Low flying eagles'. You might develop the game further by thinking of road signs for a spiritual journey.

GUESS THE MODE OF TRANSPORT

You will need: cards with modes of transport written on them.

You can play this as a mime game like charades. The children take it in turns to take a card and mime the mode of transport until someone guesses what it might be. Be imaginative with this as well as thinking of the obvious. For example, as well as thinking of car, bus, and so on, try waterskiing, paragliding, and so on.

PRAYERS

POSTCARDS

You will need: blank postcards; pens; colouring pencils.

Talk to the children about how spiritual journeys are often seen as parallel to physical journeys. When we travel on holiday, we often send postcards. Invite the children to send a postcard to God, perhaps telling him about where they are or where they are travelling to, perhaps telling him what they hope for. They could draw a picture on the other side. If you wished, you could draw a parallel between this activity and Paul's writing of numerous letters giving spiritual support to young churches while he travelled around the Mediterranean.

COMPASS PRAYER

You will need: a compass; a map; paper; a pencil or pen.

With the children, have a look at a compass and show them how the needle works by always pointing north. Explain that using a compass with a map will help us to find out where we are and get to where we want to go. Invite them to think about how God helps us to find the way in our spiritual lives, too. Finally, invite the children to ask God to help them to find the right way to him. Now draw a circle and the four points of the compass (north, south, east and west). Notice how the four points form the shape of a cross.

MAPPING OUT PRAYER

You will need: a map (either world or local); postcards from round the world (optional).

If you have a world map, use it as inspiration to think of places in the world that need our prayers. If you wish, you could pin or stick your prayers on to the appropriate place. Alternatively, you could think about people you know who have travelled (on holiday or business) to the places you can find on the map. Maybe you know people who live in faraway places for whom you could pray. If you have any postcards, find the places where they came from on the map. If you have thought about staple foods in different parts of the world the previous day, find them on the map and pray for the people who grew or produced the food.

If you have a local map, think about people who might be on holiday in your area or people who normally live or work near you but are away on their holidays. For both maps, also pray for people who need some spiritual guidance or help.

DAY FIVE: ULTIMATE GOAL

God said to Moses: I am the eternal God. So tell them that the Lord, whose name is 'I Am', has sent you. This is my name for ever, and it is the name that people must use from now on.

I am Alpha and Omega, the first and the last, the beginning and the end.

KEY BIBLE FOCUS: EXODUS 3:14–15 AND REVELATION 22:13

'I AM' DISPLAY FOR THE CHURCH

You will need: prepared fabric hanging (see page 150); materials required to make the central design (see below); either fabric paints or fabric scraps in different colours; PVA glue; Hebrew letters (see page 191).

Use appliqué or paint to make the Hebrew letters for 'I am'. Add them to the centre of the hanging. The letters or the space around them could be decorated if you wish, but make sure the letters themselves still stand out.

TOTEM POLE KENNINGS

You will need: different sized cardboard boxes (stuck together) to make a totem pole; bright card; materials for writing and decorating card; PVA glue.

Talk to the children about the 'I am' sayings of Jesus that they have been looking at during the activity programme, and discuss the sayings as a whole. Talk about how the sayings might be changed or developed into kennings to create different words for God, such as 'flock-feeder', 'light-shiner', 'joy-maker', and so on. If you need more inspiration, look at the chapter on 'I am' in *The Gospels Unplugged* by Lucy Moore (Barnabas, 2002). Invite the children to make their own kennings and write them in large letters on the card. Ask them to decorate their work so that it looks really striking. Stick each kenning on to the totem pole to make a further display for church.

When the totem pole is complete, you might wish to talk to the children about the multifaceted nature of God. God can be all things to all people. Perhaps he may be something particular and special to us, but someone else may see him differently. Explain that we can see things differently but still have faith in the same God.

DISCUSSION

Talk with the children about the significance of the words 'I am' in Hebrew. This is where 'Yahweh', the Hebrew name for God, comes from.

Read Exodus 3:14–15 and Revelation 22:13. Point out that these verses come from opposite ends of the Bible, and talk about how they embrace all the others you have looked at.

CRAFT ACTIVITIES

DECORATING T-SHIRTS

> **You will need:** plain T-shirts in appropriate sizes; fabric paint; plastic carrier bags; cardboard; brushes.

Give each child a T-shirt of the appropriate size. Wrap plastic carrier bags round pieces of cardboard cut to size and carefully feed one inside each T-shirt to prevent paint from seeping through from front to back. Talk briefly about the different 'I am' sayings and then invite the children to decorate their T-shirts using fabric paint. They could depict their favourite 'I am' saying or perhaps invent one of their own. They could use words or pictures or both.

The T-shirts will need to be ironed when they are dry to fix the paint: you will need to refer to the paint manufacturer's instructions. If necessary, the children could be sent home with instructions on how to fix the paint.

'YOU ARE...'

> **You will need:** paper; pens.

Remind the children of the 'I am' sayings and tell them that it is now their turn to think of their own ways to describe what God is like. Take them through writing a poem line by line. (There is an example of a poem written in this way in the 'Prayers' section below.) Ask the children to think about what God would be if he were a colour (they will need to be specific and also think of a reason). Encourage them to keep their thoughts brief and condensed. Ask them to write down the colour as the first line of a poem beginning 'You are...' . Next, invite them to think about what God would be if he were a plant, a building, a musical instrument, a sport, a form of water, or anything else you might think of. When the children have written these lines, ask them to choose the three or four best lines to form their final poem.

If you want to make a group compilation poem, pick the best lines as a joint effort to get the best poem you can. You could write this up and put it on display, publish it in your parish magazine or just use it for prayer.

GAMES

GOAL!

> **You will need:** a large table; masking tape; a table tennis ball.

Mark the table into thirds with two lines of masking tape and designate the two end areas as the 'goals'. Players must stand behind their goals but may reach over the table to stop the ball. The object is for each player to score a goal in their opponent's goal. Use a table tennis ball, or something of similar size but a little heavier. Players can roll, push or flick the ball, but it mustn't be picked up and thrown. When players move the ball, it must be in contact with the table.

'YOU ARE...' POEM

> **You will need:** a 'You are…' poem.

If you have written a 'You are…' poem, use it as a starter for prayer. If you need more inspiration, you could use the prayer below as an example.

> *You are blue as the shimmering ocean reflecting beautiful sky.*
> *You are the dazzling rainbow on a beautiful spring morning.*
>
> *You are the tallest, most beautiful sunflower.*
>
> *You are a stable; a small cottage;*
> *You are a home to be special and happy in.*
>
> *You are an orchestra playing the quietness of a mouse*
> *and the loudness of a lion.*
> *You are a sweet singing voice like birds in the trees.*
>
> *You are a wave overpowering evil; you are the soft rain;*
> *You are a rippling stream; you are the saving water we drink.*
> *Amen*
>
> SAPLINGS' COMPILATION POEM TO GOD

ALPHA AND OMEGA

Use a symbolic object for the children to pass round, to inspire either private or spoken prayers. You could consider using:

★ A ring or small hoop to symbolize eternity or the perfection of God
★ A model alpha and omega
★ A symbol of the Trinity
★ A simple cross

Something may have come out of your discussions which will have resonance with the children and will help sum up the series of workshops.

APPENDICES

Appendix 1

SAMPLE PROGRAMME PLAN

Programme plans for all sessions, with age bandings, can be found at www.barnabasinchurches.org.uk/throughtheyearwithjesus.

Plan 2 (children aged 7–12)

TIME	ACTIVITY	MATERIALS
10 minutes	Registration	Pen; paper; registration forms; badges
10 minutes	Visual storytelling	Visual materials, such as a blue cloth, bread and stone, a scroll, a toy snake and a model or picture of a church building
10 minutes	Painting shells	Scallop shells; acrylic paint; brushes; water
15 minutes	Marbling	Paper; tray of water; marbling ink
15 minutes	Oil pastel pictures	Pastels; paper
10 minutes	BREAK	Squash; biscuits; cups; jugs; water
10 minutes	Jesus' baptism	Child's storytelling Bible or contemporary version of the Bible
20 minutes	Illuminated names	Name book to look up meanings of names; paint; ink and brushes, or pens; paper
10 minutes	Praying with water	Font or glass bowl; water

Reproduced with permission from *Through the Year with Jesus!* published by BRF 2009 (978 1 84101 578 1)
www.barnabasinchurches.org.uk

TEMPLATES

DOVE MOBILES

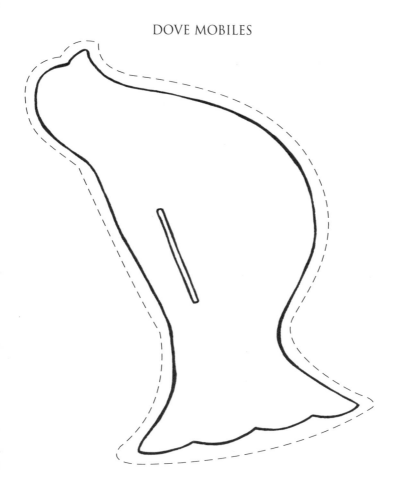

Reproduced with permission from *Through the Year with Jesus!* published by BRF 2009 (978 1 84101 578 1)
www.barnabasinchurches.org.uk

STAINED-GLASS WINDOW CANDLES

Reproduced with permission from *Through the Year with Jesus!* published by BRF 2009 (978 1 84101 578 1)
www.barnabasinchurches.org.uk

ACORN BADGES

Reproduced with permission from *Through the Year with Jesus!* published by BRF 2009 (978 1 84101 578 1)
www.barnabasinchurches.org.uk

185

PAPER CHAIN PEOPLE

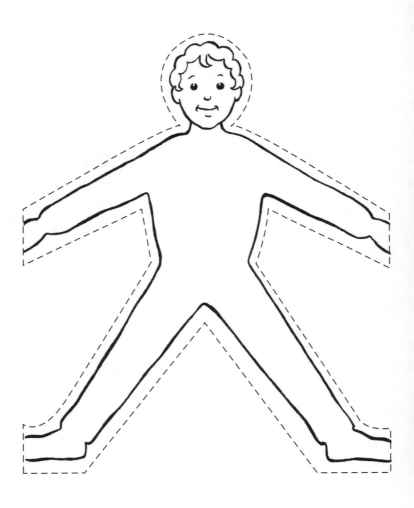

Reproduced with permission from *Through the Year with Jesus!* published by BRF 2009 (978 1 84101 578 1)
www.barnabasinchurches.org.uk

COCKEREL FEATHER COLLAGE

Reproduced with permission from *Through the Year with Jesus!* published by BRF 2009 (978 1 84101 578 1)
www.barnabasinchurches.org.uk

TESSELLATING BIRDS

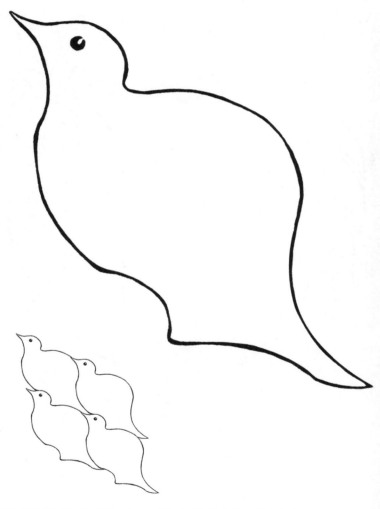

ACTIVITY FIGURES

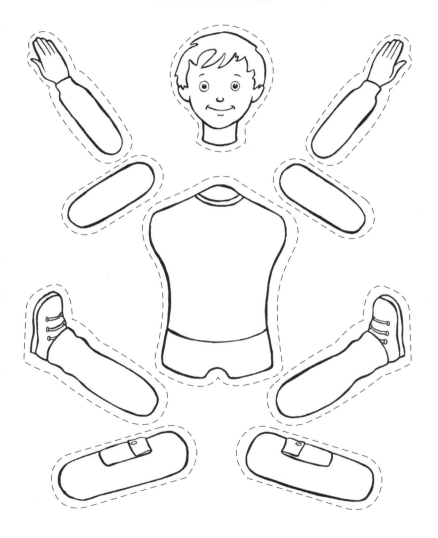

'I AM' DISPLAY: WORLD STENCIL

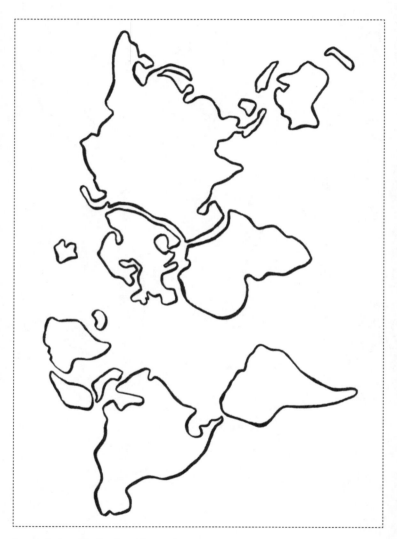

SHEEP FRIEZE

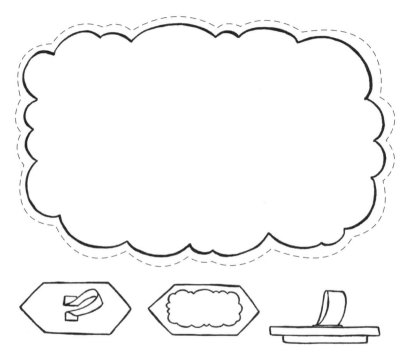

'I AM' DISPLAY: HEBREW LETTERS

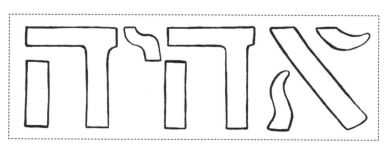

Reproduced with permission from *Through the Year with Jesus!* published by BRF 2009 (978 1 84101 578 1)
www.barnabasinchurches.org.uk

BIBLIOGRAPHY

Listed below are the resources used directly for this book and the original workshops, as well as those that have inspired ideas. A diverse selection of Bible translations is recommended when trying to find the right language for a particular story (it won't always be the children's version).

Alongside Christian resources, general children's activity books often contain ideas that can be adapted to illustrate a Christian story.

BIBLES AND BIBLE STORIES

The Dramatised Bible (Marshall Pickering, 1989)

The Lion Children's Bible (Lion, 1981)

International Children's Bible (Nelson Word, 1983)

Contemporary English Version of the Bible (HarperCollins, 2000)

New Revised Standard Version (HarperCollins, 1989)

The Barnabas Children's Bible (Barnabas, 2007)

The Children's Illustrated Bible (Dorling Kindersley, 1994)

The Usborne Children's Bible (Usborne Publishing, 2000)

My Book of Bible Stories (Lion, 2002)

Stories Jesus Told, Nick Butterworth and Mick Inkpen (Marshall Pickering, 1996)

CHRISTIAN RESOURCE BOOKS

Godly Play, Jerome W. Berryman (Augsburg, 1991)

Young Children and Worship, Sonya M. Stewart and Jerome W. Berryman (Westminster John Knox Press, 1989)

Following Jesus, Sonya M. Stewart and Jerome W. Berryman (Geneva Press, 2000)

Teaching Godly Play, Sonya M. Stewart and Jerome W. Berryman (Abingdon Press, 1995)

The Complete Guide to Godly Play, Volumes 1–6, Jerome W. Berryman (Living the Good News, 2002–2006)

Theme Games, Lesley Pinchbeck (Scripture Union, 1993)

Theme Games 2, Lesley Pinchbeck (Scripture Union, 2002)

Festive Allsorts: Ideas for Celebrating the Christian Year, Nicola Currie (National Society/Church House Publishing, 1994)

Seasons and Saints for the Christian Year, Nicola and Stuart Currie (National Society/Church House Publishing, 1998)

The 'E' Book: Essential prayers and activities for faith at home, Gill Ambrose (National Society/Church House Publishing, 2000)

Children Aloud, Gordon and Ronni Lamont (National Society/Church House Publishing, 1997)

One Hundred and One Ideas for Creative Prayers, Judith Merrell (Scripture Union, 1995)

New Ideas for Creative Prayer, Judith Merrell (Scripture Union, 2001)

The Gospels Unplugged, Lucy Moore (Barnabas, 2002)

The Lord's Prayer Unplugged, Lucy Moore (Barnabas, 2004)

Here's One I Made Earlier, Kathryn Copsey (Scripture Union, 1995)

Here's Another One I Made Earlier, Christine Orme (Scripture Union, 2000)

Come and Join the Celebration, John Muir and Betty Pedley (National Society Enterprises/Church House Publishing, 2001)

Welcome to the Lord's Table, Margaret Withers (Barnabas, 1999)

A Child's Book of Saints, Christopher Doyle (Barnabas, 2009)

Sounds of the Eternal, J. Philip Newell (Canterbury Press, 2002)

Woven into Prayer, Angela Ashwin (Canterbury Press, 1999)

CHILDREN'S ACTIVITY BOOKS

Festive Fun, Gillian Souter (Off the Shelf Publishing, 2001)

Fun to Make, Gillian Souter (Off the Shelf Publishing, 2001)

Beads and Badges, Gillian Souter (Off the Shelf Publishing, 1999)

Cool Stuff, Susie Lacome (MQ Publications, 2002)

Play Together, Learn Together, Melanie Rice (Kingfisher Books, 1985)

Fun to Make and Do, Hannah Tofts and Annie Owen (Two-Can Publishing, 1990)

Making Presents, Juliet Bawden (Hamlyn, 1993)

What Shall I Draw?, Ray Gibson (Usborne, 2002)

Make and Colour Paper Planes, Clare Beaton (b small publishing, 2000)

OTHER RESOURCES

500 Fabulous Cakes and Bakes (Anness, 1996, 2006)

The English Poems of George Herbert, ed. C.A. Patrides (J.M. Dent, 1974)

Harry and the Bucketful of Dinosaurs, Ian Whybrow and Adrian Reynolds (David and Charles, 1999)

How to Eat: The Pleasures and Principles of Good Food, Nigella Lawson (Chatto and Windus, 1998)

A Revelation of Love, Julian of Norwich, ed. Marion Glasscoe (University of Exeter, 1976)

Wonderful Earth!, Nick Butterworth and Mick Inkpen (Hunt and Thorpe, 1991)

MUSIC

'Jesus' blood never failed me yet', Gavin Bryars (Philips, 1993)

WEBSITES

www.bbc.co.uk
www.scoutingresources.org.uk
www.activityvillage.co.uk
www.barnabasinchurches.org.uk

NOT SUNDAY, NOT SCHOOL!

THROUGH-THE-YEAR CHILDREN'S PROGRAMMES FOR SMALL CHURCHES

Many churches, particularly those with small congregations and even smaller numbers of children attending on a Sunday morning, struggle with the traditional model of Sunday school and long to find a way to work with more children more effectively. This book sets out to show that, with a bit of lateral and creative thinking, perceived weaknesses can become strengths, with the end result that children's work, even in a small church, can become vibrant and successful.

Not Sunday, Not School! is packed with ideas and activities for an alternative model to the traditional Sunday school. The material comprises tried and tested two-hour thematic programmes that will take you right the way through the Christian year, plus an alternative programme for Hallowe'en and a series for a five-day holiday club programme, or stand-alone workshops for the summer months.

Each session includes suggestions for Bible stories based on the theme, suggestions for creating a display for the church, craft activities, games and suggestions for prayer.

ISBN 978 1 84101 490 6   £9.99
Available from your local Christian bookshop or, in case of difficulty, direct from BRF using the order form on page 199.

MESSY CHURCH

FRESH IDEAS FOR BUILDING
A CHRIST-CENTRED COMMUNITY

LUCY MOORE

Messy Church is bursting with easy-to-do ideas to draw people of all ages together and help them to experience what it means to be part of a Christian community outside of Sunday worship. The book sets out the theory and practice of Messy Church and offers 15 themed programme ideas to get you started, each including Bible references and background, art and craft activities, recipes and family-friendly worship outlines.

'... crammed with good things... delights on every page... full of good fun, deep wisdom and practical know-how. Messy Church will be a blessing to many. I hope it leads to lots of mess and to many different forms of church.'
FROM THE FOREWORD BY THE REVD DR STEVEN CROFT

ISBN 978 1 84101 503 3   £8.99
Available from your local Christian bookshop or, in case of difficulty, direct from BRF using the order form on page 199.

See the following pages for an extract from *Messy Church*— 'Abraham and Sarah', the first unit in a thematic programme on 'God's family, our family'.

Abraham and Sarah

AIM

To see that we all belong to the same family of believers, which started with the story of Abraham and Sarah and God's promise to them.

BIBLE BACKGROUND (Genesis 12—21)

This is a huge, epic story but we've simplified it down to a few elements. God calls Abram to go on a journey with him. His wife Sarai can't have children and this makes them very sad. On the journey, God promises Abram that he will have more children than there are stars in the sky or grains of sand in the desert. As a sign of that promise, God changes Abram's name to Abraham and Sarai's name to Sarah.

God's promise comes true when Sarah finally does have a baby, called Isaac, when she's very old. The great-great-great-(lots of greats)-grandchildren of this family are the members of God's family here today, so we are all members of the same family—God's family of believers. God's promise starts with small things but can become incredibly massive.

FOOD

Pasta plus

Serve up the pasta and peas from the kitchen. Have bowls of sauce and bowls of grated cheese on the tables to be dished up there by parents or teenagers. It takes too long to put everything on a plate in the kitchen and to get it out to people hot.

ACTIVITIES

Printing stars

You will need: Craft sponges (from Early Learning Centre or similar), waxy potatoes (washed and dried), pots of poster paint in different colours, dark paper or card

Use the sponges or potatoes cut into star shapes with at least three colours of paint. Print the stars on to dark paper or card.

Talk about
During this activity, talk about how many stars you can see in the night sky and encourage everyone to count them tonight.

'Sand' bottles

You will need: A variety of different-coloured beads or coloured 'sands' made from salt and powder poster paint (see below), clear plastic bottles

Use a variety of different-coloured beads or coloured 'sands' to fill clear plastic bottles with layers of different colours. Seal them tightly!

You can make 'sand' with salt and poster paint. For sand colour, add a teaspoon of yellow and half a teaspoon of red paint to a 1 kg bag of salt.

Talk about

During this activity, talk about counting the grains of sand in the bottles and how the numbers just go on and on. Ask what the biggest number is that they can think of. Marvel together at the idea of infinity.

Family cards

> **You will need**: Mediumweight white or coloured card, stickers, punches, coloured scraps and so on, PVA glue, scissors, coloured pens or pencils

Design a card to give to someone you love in your family, maybe living near you or maybe far away. Use stickers, punches and coloured scraps to make it look beautiful.

Talk about

Talk about the way families go back and back and back in time, from parents to grandparents and great-grandparents to even further back. Expect to hear lots about elderly relatives! Talk about how one day the children might be parents or grandparents or great-grandparents themselves! Family stretches out across time.

Warhammer workshop

> **You will need**: Warhammer models (encourage the children to bring in their collections), enamel paints in different colours, small brushes, jars of cleaner, kitchen paper

Have fun painting the models together!

Talk about
Talk about the fun of collecting things, looking after our collections and seeing them grow.

Watercolour faces

You will need: Watercolour paints in different colours, watercolour paper, paintbrushes, jars of clean water, kitchen paper

Use watercolours to paint a face on a small piece of watercolour paper.

Talk about
Talk about the different colours that go into making the whole picture, just like different people go into making up a whole family.

Journeys

You will need: Prepared outlines of cars, trains, camels, horses and caravans (drawn in thick marker pen on paper), poster paints in different colours, paint brushes, jars of clean water, kitchen paper

Using your prepared outlines, invite everyone to paint their family on a journey using one of these means of transport. Encourage them to add extended family, church family and friends.

Talk about
Talk about journeys that families have to make sometimes. Has anyone made a journey with his or her family recently? How was it? How did they manage when they all wanted to go in different directions?

Star mobiles

> **You will need:** Cardboard star shapes, glitter and glitter glue, shiny gift ribbon, wire coathangers

Decorate cardboard star shapes with glitter and glitter glue, and hang them on shiny gift ribbon from a wire coathanger.

Talk about
Talk about the stars in the sky that are there even in the day when we can't see them. Each one of them is different.

Star sticking

> **You will need:** Sheets of dark paper, tubes of shiny silver stars, PVA glue, silver or gold pens

On dark paper, use shiny silver stars to create your own constellation, and give it a name.

Talk about
Talk about the patterns the stars make in the sky and how people have seen animals, birds and heroes in the constellations.

Sand tray

> **You will need:** A sandpit or sandtray filled with silver sand, seaside buckets, scoops and spoons

Have a sandpit or sandtray to play in, with buckets, scoops and spoons.

Talk about

Talk about the desert and how it's always changing as the wind blows on it. Talk about the seaside and making sandcastles and sandpies.

Ziggurat sandwiches

You will need: Slices of thin white bread, various sandwich fillings, table knives, paper plates

Have slices of thin white bread, ready cut into different-sized squares, and various sandwich fillings: jam, cheese, ham, yeast extract, lettuce, chocolate spread, sandwich spread and so on. Make ziggurats by sandwiching the squares of bread together in ever-decreasing sizes with different fillings until you have made a pyramid-shaped edifice. You may or may not want to eat it...

Talk about

Talk about the ancient city of Ur, where people worshipped nature gods in buildings called ziggurats, and how Abraham met the true God not in a building but out in the desert.

CELEBRATION

Setting up the church or worship space

You will need: Large cardboard stars, PowerPoint loaded with digital pictures of finished artwork (optional), samples of artwork from each activity station, small bowl of silver sand

Put large cardboard stars out on the floor and hang more wherever possible. If you are using PowerPoint, have this ready to display photos of artwork as everyone comes in.

Song selection

I reach up high (*Kidsource 1*, 171)
Any kind of weather (Doug Horley, *Humungous Song Book*, 2)
Faith as small as a mustard seed (Doug Horley, *Humungous Song Book*, 15)
Have we made our God too small? (Doug Horley, *Humungous Song Book*, 23)

Talk

Looking at the artwork, I see lots of sand and lots of stars. It reminds me of a story.

Use pictures loaded into PowerPoint or samples of artwork from each activity station to tell the story.

There was a man called Abraham. He was very old and he was married to Sarah. They were very sad because they had no children.

But one night, out in the desert, God made Abraham a special promise. God said to Abraham, 'Look up and count the stars—if you can. That's how many people there will be in your family one day…'

Show PowerPoint image or artwork sample of stars.

'… Think of the sand on the seashore. How many grains can you count?

I'll bless you and give you such a large family that one day they'll be as many as the stars in the sky or the grains of sand on the seashore.'

Pick up the bowl of sand and let the sand run through your fingers into the bowl.

God kept his promise. We're Abraham's family, because we're God's family—the Christian family of faith. We've millions of brothers and sisters of all ages and colours in every land all over the world.

Prayer response

Encourage everyone to think of something to thank God for. Ask them to put up their hand to say what that thing is. As people give their response, repeat it and invite everyone to say, 'Lord God, we thank you.'

Final blessing

Lord, thank you that we are one big family of your people throughout the world and throughout history. Help us to live as one family, loving each other through thick and thin. Amen

Messy Grace

May the grace of our Lord Jesus Christ (*Hold out your hands as if expecting a present*)
And the love of God (*Put your hands on your heart*)
And the fellowship of the Holy Spirit (*Hold hands*)
Be with us all now and for ever. Amen! (*Raise hands together on the word 'Amen'*)

MESSY CHURCH 2

IDEAS FOR DISCIPLING
A CHRIST-CENTRED COMMUNITY

LUCY MOORE

Messy Church is growing! Since it began in 2004, many churches have picked up the idea of drawing people of all ages together and inviting them to experience fun-filled Christian community outside Sunday worship.

Following the popular Messy Church formula, *Messy Church 2* not only provides a further 15 exciting themed sessions, but also explores ways to help adults and children alike to go further and deeper with God—in other words, to grow as disciples. As before, the material is overflowing with ideas for creativity, fun, food, fellowship and family-friendly worship, but new to *Messy Church 2* are 'take-away' ideas to help people think about their Messy Church experience between the monthly events.

ISBN 978 1 84101 602 3   £8.99
Available from your local Christian bookshop or, in case of difficulty, direct from BRF using the order form on page 199.

ORDER FORM

REF	TITLE	PRICE	QTY	TOTAL
490 6	*Not Sunday, Not School!*	£9.99		
503 3	*Messy Church*	£8.99		
602 3	*Messy Church 2*	£8.99		

POSTAGE AND PACKING CHARGES					
Order value	UK	Europe	Surface	Air Mail	Postage and packing:
£7.00 & under	£1.25	£3.00	£3.50	£5.50	Donation:
£7.01–£30.00	£2.25	£5.50	£6.50	£10.00	**Total enclosed:**
Over £30.00	free	prices on request			

Name _____ Account Number _____

Address_____

_____ Postcode _____

Telephone Number _____ Email _____

Payment by: ❏ Cheque ❏ Mastercard ❏ Visa ❏ Postal Order ❏ Maestro

Card no. ☐☐☐☐ ☐☐☐☐ ☐☐☐☐ ☐☐☐☐

Expires ☐☐ ☐☐   Security code ☐☐☐   Issue no. ☐☐☐

Signature _____ Date _____

All orders must be accompanied by the appropriate payment.

Please send your completed order form to:
BRF, 15 The Chambers, Vineyard, Abingdon OX14 3FE
Tel. 01865 319700 / Fax. 01865 319701 Email: enquiries@brf.org.uk

❏ Please send me further information about BRF publications.

Available from your local Christian bookshop.   BRF is a Registered Charity

Resourcing people to work with 3–11s
in churches and schools

- Articles, features, ideas
- Training and events
- Books and resources
- www.barnabasinchurches.org.uk